Family Ministry BASICS

CONCORDIA PUBLISHING HOUSE · SAINT LOUIS

Basics

Edited by Mark S. Sengele

Unless otherwise indicated, all Scripture quotations are from The Holy Bible, English Standard Version®. Copyright © 2001 by Crossway Bibles, publishing ministry of Good News Publishers, Wheaton, Illinois. Used by permission. All rights reserved.

Scripture quotations marked NIV are taken from the HOLY BIBLE, NEW INTERNATIONAL VERSION®. NIV®. Copyright © 1973, 1978, 1984 by International Bible Society. Used by permission of Zondervan Publishing House. All rights reserved.

The quotation marked LW is from Luther's Works, American Edition, vol. 45, copyright © 1962 Fortress Press.

Catechism quotations are taken from Luther's Small Catechism with Explanation, copyright © 1986, 1991 Concordia Publishing House.

The Catholic Catechism quotation is taken from The Catechism of the Catholic Church Second Edition, © 1994 United States Catholic Conference, Inc. Used by permission.

This publication may be available in braille, in large print, or on cassette tape for the visually impaired. Please allow 8 to 12 weeks for delivery. Write to the Library for the Blind, 7550 Watson Rd., St. Louis, MO 63119-4409; call toll-free 1-888-215-2455; or visit the Web site: www.blindmission.org.

Your comments and suggestions concerning the material are appreciated. Please write the Editor of Youth Materials, Concordia Publishing House, 3558 S. Jefferson Avenue, St. Louis, MO 63118–3968.

Manufactured in the United States of America

1 2 3 4 5 6 7 8 9 10   15 14 13 12 11 10 09 08 07 06

Table of Contents

1. Why Family Ministry?   4
JEFFERY S. SCHUBERT

2. The Marriage Connection   13
BRYAN SALMINEN

3. Defining Family   25
ROGER SONNENBERG

4. Getting Started: A Blueprint for Congregational Family Ministry   34
STEVE AND DEE CHRISTOPHER

5. Relationships: Dealing with Marriage and Each Person's Role in the Family   44
JOHN W. OBERDECK

6. Touchpoints: Identifying Opportunities to Minister *with* Families   53
CRAIG S. OLDENBURG

7. Generations   63
HARRY KRUPSKY

8. GRANDparenting   71
RICH BIMLER

9. Passing on the Faith   78
AUDREY DUENSING-WERNER

10. Family Ministry Celebrations   86
KAY MEYER

11. Building a Support Network   97
JILL HASSTEDT

Resources   110

BASICS

Family Ministry

table of contents

Why Family Ministry?

BY JEFFERY S. SCHUBERT

Where You Came from Determines Who You Are

When you hear the cliché "The apple never falls far from the tree," what does that bring to mind? Or how about another cliché—"Like father, like son" or "She's just like her mother"? Most of us probably think about the fact that we (like it or not!) often grow up to be similar to our parents. Consciously (or, more likely, subconsciously) we, as adults, often display characteristics from the family that reared us. The line "He'd grown up just like me, my boy was just like me," hauntingly sung by Harry Chapin in his classic "Cats in the Cradle," contains more truth than we'd like to admit.

In the 1960s, a television commercial included the jingle "You can take Salem out of the country, but you can't take the country out of Salem." That commercial gave viewers the impression that smoking a Salem would bestow that country-fresh feeling.

This advertising tagline gives us insight into an important fact about families. "You can take a person out of his family, but you can't take that family out of the person." Social scientists talk in terms of "family of origin" and "socialization within the family system," using clinical terms and psychological research. But the conclusion is the same: Where you come from (your family of origin) often determines the person you ultimately become.

For my wife and me, the family system reality check came down to the day we would celebrate Christmas. You see, my wife was raised with the tradition of opening gifts on Christmas Day morning, a tradition established in her psyche long before she met me. Conversely, my family opened gifts on Christmas Eve, again, a deeply valued tradition. Early in our marriage, we worked out a lot of our "family of origin" differences, but this one awaited until December 24 to surface.

It was after Christmas Eve church services, and I was ready to open gifts. Of course, my wife stopped me in mid-tear of the paper. "What are you doing?" she asked incredulously. "Opening my gifts," I said innocently, somewhat amazed that she would even need to ask. It was, of course, the 24th of December, after church!

"No, we open gifts tomorrow morning," she corrected. "That is, after all, the correct day to do it." And then she expounded on how Santa comes down the chimney on Christmas Eve while we are asleep, and in the morning we would all be surprised by the gifts under the tree.

I countered with the birth of Jesus. We celebrate His birth on Christmas Eve, and since our Lord was the greatest gift of all, we should celebrate by opening our gifts the same night. I underscored my point by also reminding her that we were adults now and neither of us still believed in Santa Claus.

But my best efforts in the "defense of Christmas Eve openings" were in vain. She was adamant. Finally, the truth spilled out: "But that's how my family always did it!" *Aha!* Family of origin! I knew it. "Well, honey, *my* family did it on Christmas Eve." We finally "agreed to disagree" on the matter and gave each other permission to celebrate in our own way. I got to open my gifts that night; she was to open hers the next morning.

That style of conflict resolution was fine until my wife saw the fun I was having opening my gifts immediately. Meanwhile, hers sat there wrapped and ignored in a pile under the tree. "You know," she observed somewhat philosophically, "it really doesn't matter *when* you open gifts, does it?" "No, it doesn't," I nodded in agreement. "There's nothing in the Bible about it." "Well, then," she said, eyeing her gifts, "I think it wouldn't be fair for you to open your gifts all alone!"

Most gracious of her, I thought, *allowing me to save face like that.* And so, with a flourish, she began to open her gifts and, in so doing, discarded a piece of her inbred family of origin traditions. Ever since then our family, including the kids, has always opened Christmas gifts on Christmas Eve. Because, as any of them will tell you, "That is the *correct* time to open them." Long live family traditions!

The Lasting Impact of Family of Origin

What we learned in our families seems to stay with us, doesn't it? The influence of the family is far-reaching and often spans generations. One's family of origin molds how we view life, what we value, the traditions we hold sacred, what we believe, how we manage money, and even how we solve disagreements. Through time and experience our families have given us our worldview, our feelings about ourselves, and our confidence (or lack of it) in facing our own future. Family ultimately shapes who we are, instilling our knowledge of right and wrong, personal ethics, the way we communicate, and how we show emotion. Most important, for Christians, our family proves very influential in passing on the Christian faith from one generation to the next.

We hear so much today about the impact of the media on our children. We are rightly concerned about what our children learn in the classroom, what they experience on the Internet, and who their peers are. But as research has shown, time and time again, the most influential factor in the lives of children are their moms and dads—the family system in which they were raised. The adage "The apple never falls far from the tree" is more than a cliché.

As a pastor, I witnessed the truth of this in my confirmation classes. The students who came from families that placed a high priority on church attendance and involvement ended up becoming adults who likewise attended church regularly and were involved in parish activities. But children raised in families that attended only on Christmas and Easter and were not involved in anything unfortunately emulated the same worship patterns when they themselves grew up. So, it would seem that one generation does indeed pass along its values to the next. If the adults in a family are biblically illiterate then, unfortunately, the children may grow up to be as well.

Thankfully, however, there are exceptions to this principle. You can probably think of some individuals you know who grew up in horrendous family situations, marked with abuse and poverty, dysfunction of all sorts. Yet, despite the odds against them, they grew up to become doctors or scientists or great leaders in a variety of fields. Sadly, those individuals are usually the exception to the rule. The family of origin strongly influences the future. Because of that, it is important that the family remains a strong institution. It is critical that your family serve as a "grace place in an anxious world." Your family should be a place where children see Christian values lived out and where they learn about their Savior. Even more important, young people in your family need to experience the unconditional love and acceptance found through the free gift of faith in Christ Jesus.

The Family as the Basic Building Block

It has been said that the family is the basic building block of society. That simple statement has far-reaching implications! If the family is indeed the basic building block of society, it stands to reason that if we have weak families, we will have weak churches. If we have weak families, we will have weak towns, cities, and states. So, then, it would follow, that if we want strong, vibrant, and healthy communities, churches, and institutions, then we must seek to strengthen and support that most basic building block of them all—the family.

Our own Dr. Martin Luther, in his "Estate of Marriage," wrote:

Most certainly father and mother are apostles, bishops, and priests to their children, for it is they who make them acquainted with the Gospel. In short, there is no greater or nobler authority on earth than that of parents over their children, for this authority is both spiritual and temporal. Whoever teaches the Gospel is truly a bishop or apostle. (LW 45:46)

Likewise Moses, in the Old Testament, instructed the people of Israel,

Love the LORD your God with all your heart and with all your soul and with all your strength. These commandments that I give you today are to be upon your hearts. Impress them on your children. Talk about them when you sit at home and when you walk along the road, when you lie down and when you get up. Tie them as symbols on your hands and bind them on your foreheads. Write them on the doorframes of your houses and on your gates. (Deuteronomy 6:5–9 NIV)

Family, the basic building block of society, is critical. And how the family fares in the future will ultimately determine how all society, and even our world itself, goes.

What Is "A Family" After All?

As our world has grown more complex, more politically correct, and more inclusive, have you noticed that when you now say the word *family*, not everyone is defining it in the same way? When some hear the word *family*, they think in terms of a mother and father, some children, perhaps a family pet, and an SUV. But that family definition is only one of many in the twenty-first century. We are aware, and have been for some time, that there are many other kinds of families in our world.

There are the blended or "step" families, single-parent families, and children being raised by a grandparent. We also see spiritually mixed families, interracial households, gay and lesbian homes, and cohabitating couples. Serial marriages result in children being raised by three or four sets of parents prior to adulthood, adoptive households, or extended family homes. The list could go on and on; it seems "family" comes in all shapes and sizes.

Thus, attempting to define family becomes a perilous task, ripe for contentious debate. Each of us carries our own perceptions of what a family should properly be. And while a case can be made *for* or *against* some forms of family, the bottom line is simple—whether we like it or not, many varieties of homes exist out there. You can read more about family systems in chapter 3.

The debate about what is or what is not a family is somewhat pointless. Maybe it has significance for politicians, legislators, or those who deal with governmental assistance, taxation, or legal matters. But for those who work in the field of family ministry, debating what is or is not a family is no longer relevant. The fact remains: there are many households—families—in today's society. We must simply accept that at face value.

In Scripture, we also see many forms of family, beginning with our first family, Adam and Eve. But as sin continued its rapid and ugly spread throughout our human family, we see multitudes of changes in the family throughout the Bible.

The Book of Genesis, however, clearly shows that marriage and family, by God's initial design, from the very beginning of life, was straightforward: one man and one woman in a monogamous relationship for the duration of their earthly life. This monogamous relationship exists for the purpose of companionship, support, and procreation of children. That was how it was designed to be in the Creator's perfect and sinless world.

Genesis also recounts mankind's terrible fall into sin. When sin entered our world, along with it came not only death (physical and spiritual), but also permutations of all God's creation, including His design for marriage and the family. So it shouldn't surprise us that as time marches on, and with each succeeding generation, there is a continual progression away from what God originally intended for families.

To become embroiled in a debate regarding the definition of family is nonproductive. Scholars, politicians, social scientists, and psychologists can pontificate as long as they wish. And certainly the Church's strong and clear voice should be heard on what Scripture says about the matter. I don't mean to imply that the Church should be silent when it comes to the matter of proper definition, especially those that relate to what marriage and family are all about.

That said, however, we must likewise be clear that when it comes to *ministry* to families, we no longer have the luxury to pick and choose those to whom we must minister. Granted, we might be uncomfortable with some family forms and perhaps even think, *That's not a family in my book,* but nevertheless it is a household God has called us to serve. So rather than define or analyze what constitutes a family, I would hold that it is more important to get out there and proclaim to those homes the Gospel of Jesus Christ and His Good News of blood-bought forgiveness and eternal life. Because while it may be true that one size doesn't fit all, all do, in fact, need one thing—the Good News of Jesus Christ.

Under Satan's Siege and in Need of Reinforcements

We know the forces working against strong and intact families. Statistics and research have sounded the alarm for years. Counseling offices continue to be packed with unhappy spouses and troubled families. Divorce statistics have not changed appreciably for years. Households continue their struggle under tight finances, lack of time, and the tyranny of the urgent. Living in our day causes considerable stress upon all our family members. So it shouldn't surprise us when we hear of spousal or child abuse, alcohol and drug problems, sexual dysfunctions, infidelity, unresolved conflict, communication breakdowns, teenage rebellion, divorce, and the pain of broken and hurting families.

It would be wonderful to say that Christian homes are immune from such issues. But, as we must sadly confess, they are not. In fact, Christian homes experience many of the same things that non-Christian homes do. Satan does not take a holiday when it comes to attacking Christian homes. No, indeed, he attacks our homes even harder, as any church leader can tell you.

Family ministry (also known as family life education) has been around for a long time. But in recent times, it would seem that it has taken a new prominence in Christian circles. Our congregations are increasingly concerned that their families are not healthy. Churches are troubled that homes in their parish are breaking apart at record numbers. Church leaders want to know what, if anything, they can do about it.

We can quote statistics. We can study Census Bureau data. We can track divorces. But when all is said and done, the conclusion is simple: The family is most certainly under satanic siege. Our homes need immediate help. The time for wringing our hands is over. We can sit around a committee table and commiserate, saying, "Isn't it awful!" We can draft reports, convene think tanks, appeal to denominational conventions, and draw up resolutions for churches to follow. But that will be about as productive as having meetings to discuss "What is a family?" All the while our families are being attacked by the enemy, and hundreds of thousands of husbands, wives, and children are being permanently wounded. The time for study is over. The time has come for serious and strategic action!

Christ to the Rescue

The Church is in a unique position to strengthen the family, whatever its form and no matter how it has been assaulted over the ages. Jesus Christ, the Lord of the Church and its Savior, came not to be served, but to serve, and to give His life as a ransom for many (Matthew 20:25–28). It didn't matter to Jesus if He were ministering to a Pharisee or a publican, a leper or a prostitute, a Roman or a Jew. What mattered to Jesus was that they were like sheep without a shepherd, lost and in need of being reunited to their Father and Creator. Jesus wasn't concerned with proper definitions or what the research said. He didn't worry about statistics or opinion polls. He just taught and healed and comforted and, yes, on occasion, even condemned the self-righteous. Yet through it all, Jesus never lost sight of His mission. He never lost sight of why He had been sent by His Father, namely, to lay down His life as a ransom for all the world's families.

Jesus gave His Church, His modern-day disciples (that's you and me!), this same search and recovery mission. We must bring the message of Jesus into all of the homes in our world, be they traditional nuclear families, single-parent households, blended families, extended families, nontraditional and, yes, even "families" that we might not call "family" in the way we normally think of that term.

God the Father would have all households be saved and to come to the knowledge of the truth. So, then, we in the Church should not differentiate either when it comes to the families who need to be touched by our congregation's Word and Sacrament ministry. As the mission statement of The Lutheran Church—Missouri Synod aptly puts it,

In grateful response to God's grace and empowered by the Holy Spirit through Word and Sacraments, the mission of The Lutheran Church—Missouri Synod is to vigorously make known the love of Christ by word and deed within our churches, communities, and the world.

What Does This Mean?

For many years, different cultures have told a fable about six blind men who set out to describe an elephant. One of the blind men took hold of the elephant's trunk and said, "I perceive the elephant to be like a snake." The man at the other end of the animal, holding the tail, said, "No, I perceive the elephant to be more like a rope." The third man, hugging the elephant's leg, stated, "Not at all. The elephant, I perceive, is more like a tree." The fourth man, feeling his way along the elephant's side, said, "No, my friends, the elephant is like a wall." The fifth man, feeling the elephant's tusk, observed, "The elephant is, alas, like a large spear." The sixth and final man exclaimed as he held the elephant's ear, "No, all of you are wrong. The elephant is like a large fan!"

We smile at this story, don't we? The conclusion is obvious. Each man had part of the picture (part of the elephant!), but no one saw just how large the entire entity was. Each was correct, but each was also wrong. Together, they would have understood. But separately, they had an erroneous perspective.

So it is when we attempt to define family ministry. As we have already discovered, *family* can mean different things to different people. Likewise, the word *ministry* has differing definitions. It may mean something as simple as offering a cup of cold water to a child in the name of Christ or as formal as the Office of the Holy Ministry! And when you put the words *family* and *ministry* together, what exactly do you mean?

Do you mean premarital education and counseling? Yes. *Do you mean marriage enrichment?* Yes. *Do you mean parenting education?* Of course! *Do you mean step-parenting training?* Yes. *How about support for those divorced or widowed or single by choice?* Yes, indeed, these things too! And we have yet to even scratch the surface when it comes to the many facets of life-span family ministry. Someone once quipped, "Doing family ministry is like hugging a whale. It's hard to get your arms around it!"

There is a general definition that may prove useful: "Family ministry is a focus on serving families regardless of their structure, as well as serving the greater family of the congregation." Another is "Family ministry is serving people wherever they are in the life cycle, whatever stage they are in, and whatever their situation happens to be." And, more recently, family proponents have stated that family ministry should be "Home centered–Church supported ministry that enables the home to be the center of faith formation."

This last definition reminds us that the Church's role should be to equip, train, and strengthen parents to be the primary agents in the faith formation of their children. Instead of the Church assuming this role for the parents, the Church rather places the responsibility for faith formation back where it rightly belongs, namely, on mom and dad.

But the Church is not just to leave them with the job! It, then, must do what is necessary to equip its parents to pass on the teachings of the faith to the children who are entrusted to their care. In so doing, the Church and the home become true partners in this unique mission of bringing up families in the fear and admonition of the Lord.

Where Do We Begin and How Is This Done?

By now I assume that you understand the influence families exert on their children and the important role the Church should play in this process. But knowing where to begin and what to do is quite another matter. When one truly begins to "unpack" this thing we call family ministry, one soon discovers just how complex it can be.

Ministry to families is a womb-to-tomb endeavor, a cradle-to-grave or life-span ministry if you will. Just think how much happens from a person's birth all the way to death! Growing up into adulthood, through those turbulent years of adolescence, into the dating years, the engagement, marriage, parenting, empty nesting, grandparenting, and maybe even great-grandparenting! Then there is the loss of a spouse and one's eventual sickness and death. Throughout life, people face all these twists and turns, the excitement and drama, and the ups and downs that come with living a long and full life.

Yet the one unchanging element throughout the life of a Christian is God's Word, written in the Scriptures and seen in the person of Jesus Christ. God's love for us in Christ never changes throughout our life span or the many permutations of family. The Church's mission is to proclaim this same eternal and unchanging grace and forgiveness found in Jesus to all families in our world, even as they continue to move and progress through the spectrum of human existence.

Basics

It's a complex job. It involves dealing with crisis. It involves providing prevention mechanisms. It involves enrichment, education, and training. It necessitates knowing the resources, products, programs, and even the correct people. It means teaching life skills. It's life-span family education at its fullest and its finest.

Anytime one sets out to master a complex task, it is extremely important to break it down into simpler, less complicated tasks—"baby steps," if you will. Take juggling, for example. You start with only one ball and master that before you move on to two balls and master that. And so it goes until one day you find yourself juggling ten balls without dropping one.

It is doubtful that after reading this book, your church will have a fully integrated, maximum functioning, seamlessly perfect ministry to every type of family in your community. The reality is that it's just too complex to expect that. But if, through the reading of this book, you discover just one or two new things that you can begin doing now to make an eternal difference in the lives of families, then this reading will not have been in vain.

As you read this book, you will be pleasantly surprised to find that this isn't rocket science. The points to keep in mind are basic: First, families are critical to the health of our society and our congregations. Second, families are the most influential institutions our children will ever encounter. Third, our families are under satanic siege. Fourth and finally, anything we can do, in the name of Christ, to strengthen, encourage, and heal homes is better than doing nothing at all or just talking about it.

Permit me a final cliché: "We must always keep the main thing the main thing." And that "main thing," of course, is Jesus Christ. We have not been called into the Church to turn it into a quasi-counseling center or into a classroom of family science or pop psychology.

We are called into the Church to faithfully proclaim Jesus Christ, crucified and risen, who alone can bring forgiveness and life to all families everywhere, by God's unfathomable mercy and grace, through the gift of faith.

And how, exactly, we in the Church can do this through family ministry will be covered in the pages that follow. Read on!

Rev. Jeffery S. Schubert serves as executive director of District and Congregational Services for The Lutheran Church—Missouri Synod.

ge Connection

e regarding the family, I would suggest that we are
e. If marriage serves as a barometer of the family
mising. Over the past three decades we've seen a signif-
e marriage ideal in our nation. A group of prominent
ed that the United States is moving from what was once
now a divorce culture. The statistics regarding divorce
ic and staggering. Six of ten marriages end in either
orce revolution creates terrible hardships for everyone
. It generates poverty within families. It burdens
costs. It fails to deliver on its promise of great adult
ships between men and women.
ment lightly. I recognize that these failures were
. The divorce revolution set out to achieve some
quality between men and women, to improve the
expand individual happiness and choice. I recognize
ese social goals.
n has not brought us closer to these goals but distances
ships between men and women are not getting

13

better—they are getting worse, becoming more difficult, more fragile, and unhappy. Too many women experience chronic economic insecurity. Too many men become isolated and estranged from their children. Too many people feel lonely and unconnected. Too many children suffer anger, sadness, and neglect.

Living in a Hopeful Time

It is time for a change because there is still hope! The Scriptures provide a divine blueprint to what marriage and the family can really be like. The Scriptures remind us that "in Christ," we are new creations and begin anew in Him. Being a child of God involves more than having "my get-out-of-jail-free card." Too many Christians make the Christian faith something nice to have when they die—a faith that keeps them out of hell, but something that does not make much apparent difference now.

Writing to the saints in Corinth, who experience one problem after another, St. Paul takes them back to the very One they have forgotten—Jesus Christ. In His resurrection, He has given them a living hope through the resurrection of the dead. Because Jesus lives, they live, not just in the future when they arrive in heaven, but now. They are forgiven their sins now and begin life as a new creation now. Of course, they don't always act new; they don't always look new; they don't always feel new. Nevertheless, Paul reminds them of something in their lives greater than their present-day experience—God! "Now faith is the assurance of things hoped for, the conviction of things not seen" (Hebrews 11:1). Faith has as its object Jesus Christ crucified and resurrected. From Him flow streams of living water. Dead marriage can be made new; dead lives, resurrected. Dead relationships can be brought back, revived, changed, and transformed; dead families, restored. These promises of the Gospel flow from God's good gifts.

The aim of this chapter is to give hope for marriage and the family. I want to share how dead, lifeless marriages, marriages that have fallen on hard times, can be resurrected. I want to emphasize that any discussion of family ministry must be connected to the health and well-being of the marriage. Based on my experience as a licensed therapist, but most important as a parish pastor, I want to impart the good news to all readers that the message of hope from the Gospel is something real and life-changing now!

This chapter is obviously and intentionally theological in nature. This chapter is not intended to be a self-help or how-to manual on marriage and the family. My training centers on marriage and family therapy and theology. I am convinced that the task of theology is learning how to interpret our lives before God, both individually and corporately. The story of God's reign continually unfolds before us, our stories unfolding with it. We must learn to share these stories because our culture supplies other stories, other narratives, that compete for the role of ordering how we think and speak, especially regarding marriage. I pray that this chapter will encourage you to take up the task of "thinking theologically" in this sense.

The plan of this chapter is as follows:

First, I want to make the case that part of the problem discussing how to minister to the family lies at the feet of the Church! I am concerned that clergy have too readily adopted a therapeutic cultural perspective rather than a theological one. I suggest that our contemporary American culture has shaped our people's understanding of marriage and the family and the clergy's as well. It is crucial that we not only understand that we are living in a divorce culture, a post-marital culture, but that we also recognize how we as clergymen have contributed to the very problem we say we want to deal with and treat. I want to challenge the reader to consider how those called to strengthen marriages have abdicated their responsibility.

Second, as theologians of the cross we say what things really are. Theologians of the cross speak the truth in all things. Regardless of current trends or conditions, theologians of the cross willingly confront life on its own terms. They take a loving but firm stand on the Word of God speaking His Word regardless of the consequences. People who look on all things through suffering and the cross are constrained to speak the truth! In other words, the theology of the cross provides the theological courage and the conceptual framework to hold the language in place and not apologize for the biblical, theological positions taken.

Third, I want to make the case that even while taking a strong stand on the Lord's Word and His will for families and marriage, it can be done in such a way as to support, love, and affirm our people. I am not suggesting that we maintain a "bludgeon the sheep" type of posture. I am suggesting that we get back to our heritage, our theological foundations, and speak what has been given to us—the Lord and His Word.

Last, I will describe and explain why we need a much bigger, better, more hopeful picture of marriage. We need a vision of the family as a place where the love of God in Christ Jesus works out in the specific details of our lives.

Looking at the Facts

Where we look for guidance about what to do about marriage and the family in the twenty-first century is as significant as it is daunting. A few decades ago, couples entered marriage with the dream of it lasting a lifetime. That dream was somewhat based in reality since many marriages did just that—last a lifetime. Even today, couples enter marriage with the notion that *their* marriage will make it despite divorce statistics. Sadly, after two or three years, the dream evaporates, and they become another statistic.

Half of all American marriages end in divorce. Most kids have one parent at home. Many marriages, even when held together, are full of tension, bitterness, resentment, and depression. Seventy-five percent of respondents to the question "If you had it to do over again, would you remarry your spouse?" said *no.* If half of all marriages end in divorce, and three-quarters of those that don't are unhappy, that means only one marriage in eight is a good one. Hey, kids, seven chances out of eight you're going to learn you can't find trust, love, security, or happiness anywhere, not even in your own home. What kind of society can be built out of those building blocks?

Today, what lasts, what endures, what really matters is no longer marriage and the family. What lasts is "autonomous self" and its emphasis on one's own feelings. The legacy left behind includes a trail of broken homes, broken lives, and broken hearts. In this "therapeutically defined universe," what matters most is not one's family or marriage, or even faith, but rather one's personal needs.

While I was serving at Concordia College in Ann Arbor, Michigan, Vice President Dan Quayle came to our campus as part of a fund-raising effort for the Concordia Family Life Institute. During his vice presidency, Mr. Quayle was stigmatized for many things, but especially his strong stand on the family and marriage. I overheard one disgruntled person say, "Everyone is talking about the family. It's the same old thing." Well, despite all the talk in Christian circles regarding the family, in our world, the focus is *not* on the family, but on the individual. People feel safe talking about keeping families together, but these same people seem afraid to stand up and say, "The way to do that is to stop divorce and keep couples together and happy." In fact, during Mr. Quayle's visit, some clergy became indignant about my position on marriage and the family. One even said, "You are taking too strong a stand on marriage. You'll offend others." While it may be the case that some people who are divorcing or contemplating divorce with no biblical grounds may be offended, I must remind myself that ultimately my responsibility is to allow the Lord to speak.

And when divorce occurs, who gets hurt the most? Kids! Attached to each of these statistics is a human face impacted by the consequences of marital breakup. Hardest hit are the children. Children of divorce are almost twice as likely to be living in poverty after the divorce. The rates of suicide, poor school performance, criminal activity, and drug abuse are significantly higher for children from broken homes than those from intact families. In fact, the situation facing children of divorce is so dire that it seems that millions of parents have purchased their own relief from marital conflict with a divorce that forces their children to pay the price in unhappiness, stress, and adjustment problems that persist a lifetime. Victimless divorce is either rare or nonexistent when children are involved.

Yet despite its prevalence and undeniable impact on everyone, there remains a strong reluctance to do anything to reverse or even slow the spread of divorce. Most scholars find the cultural attitude somewhat perplexing. If a disease were afflicting the majority of a populace, spreading pain and dysfunction throughout all age groups, we would be frantically searching for reasons and solutions. Yet this particular scourge has become so endemic that it is virtually ignored. That scourge is divorce, an oddly neglected topic in a nation that has the worst record of broken marriages in the entire world. Divorce is a root problem in our country and the cause of any number of social ills.

Instead of dealing with the actual facts on the effects of divorce, the divorce culture has now begun to propagate its own ideas regarding marriage and the family. There are two prevailing myths:

1. *Marriage and the family aren't declining; they are merely changing for the better.*

2. *Marriages are healthier and happier, children are better off, and people have more freedom now that the taboos against divorce and unwed motherhood have been overthrown.*

With these myths, the voices of intellectual and moral authority have insisted for more than a generation that there is no cause for alarm. Psychologists, marriage counselors (even pastors), college professors, and lawyers are united in insisting that divorce was better for kids and society than what they saw as the necessary alternative—a grim and hate-filled marriage.

Culturally and morally, marriage has been demoted from foundation to just another lifestyle about which neighbors, therapists, grandparents, and pastors are supposed to remain conveniently neutral in comparison to other lifestyles. The legal, social, and economic supports that sustained marriage over centuries have dispatched with astonishing speed, and marriage has been reconceived as a purely private act, not a social institution but one possible scenario, sustained entirely by and for two people for their own mutual pleasure. Thanks to "no-fault" divorce and the policies that support it, getting married today more closely resembles taking a concubine than taking a wife.

Despite these realities, people still long for marriage like never before. Over the past thirty years, a consistent 96 percent of the American public has expressed a personal desire for marriage. Only 8 percent of American women consider being single an ideal, a proportion that has not changed over the past twenty years. Almost three-fourths of adult Americans believe that marriage is a lifelong commitment that should not be ended except under extreme circumstances. Even 81 percent of divorced and separated Americans still believe that marriage should be for life.

Regardless of the political rhetoric, "family values" is a slogan without content, a politician's perfect phrase, committing no one to anything, least of all a serious agenda to restore marriage. When was the last time you heard a politician say, "Divorce is wrong"? You don't, and the reason is quite clear—we don't want to offend all the divorced people. It is important, however, to say what the Lord says. For example: just because many women have abortions does not mean that the Church should change its position that abortion is murder. Despite opposition and controversy, we remain faithful to the Word of the Lord and speak where the Lord speaks.

the marriage connection

Of course, one of the problems is how the debate on this issue has been framed. We make it sound like the debate is between choice and coercion, individual liberty and state control. "You can't force two people to stay married," we tell ourselves, and that's the end of that. But divorce is not usually the act of a couple, but of an individual. Eighty percent of divorces in this country are unilateral. The divorce revolution has not produced an increase in personal freedom but a shift in power, favoring the interests of one party over others—the interest of the spouse who wishes to leave over those of the spouse being abandoned and over children whose consent is not sought.

For too long, the collapse of marriage has been treated as a natural disaster, like typhoons, earthquakes, and tidal waves, causing pain and suffering that cannot be prevented. The best we can do in the face of this mystery, we are told, is to be like the Red Cross after a storm: go through the wreckage, pick up the survivors, and carry on. There is a lot of comfort in treating the collapse of marriage this way. If divorce and illegitimacy are inevitable, then no one needs to take responsibility for the devastation. If there is no solution, there is no problem.

The Church as Part of the Problem

It is also very important to say that the Church is part of the problem. Seventy-three percent of all first marriages are blessed by pastors, priests, or rabbis. Yet, 60 percent of all new marriages fail. Clearly, the Church has access to most marriages, but it has not taken advantage of that access following the wedding.

But somehow, many clergy and laity alike have adopted the cultural mind-set that says, "Well, divorce happens. We just can't do much about it." In the name of being kind and loving, the Church has often sold itself out to the prevailing culture. Instead of stating God's loving Word very clearly to couples in distress, pastors adopt the perspective of the divorce culture and move much too quickly to life after the divorce. "Love," of course, frames all that clergymen do. But it is not our love, but God's love in Christ for people that provides a framework for ministry. And His love for people is revealed in the Scriptures. We stand where God stands and speak where God speaks. We inform where God informs and do not apologize for taking a "thus says the Lord position" when the Lord has said "thus."

However, because divorce occurs so frequently, it becomes relatively easy to normalize it. It happens so often that we no longer are shocked by it. But we must ask, Where are those who are outraged at the scandalous behavior of, not only our leaders, but husbands and wives? Where is the outrage over families being split apart and hurt dramatically due to divorce? Does anyone even care anymore? The words of the prophet Jeremiah ring true today: "They did not know how to blush" (Jeremiah 6:15).

Recently friends of ours divorced. She's "outgrown him," she says. She doesn't like him. As she prepared for the divorce, she suddenly began to recount things that none of us had ever heard. She began to rewrite the history of the marriage, trying to suggest it had always been bad as justification for leaving the marriage. They have two teenagers who, along with my kids, have said, "This is evil."

While *evil* may sound like a harsh word, what other words can a son apply to sudden abandonment by his mother? How else could a child experience his own demotion from having one home and one set of parents to two homes and two separate and hostile parents?

But what really bothers the children and upsets me is this: Why are they, children ages 15, 13, 8, and 5, the only ones who called evil by its name? Why is it that something that by any reasonable light is destructive and wrong called up no communal response? What would have happened if everywhere she turned she was confronted by loving Christian people who said, "No, this is wrong. This is not the Lord's will, and you can make it better." Even her pastors never once told her, "This is wrong, but you need to know the good news. It can be remade."

Another couple I know recently divorced. The husband told me they went to see the pastor who said, "I'm not going to tell you not to get a divorce." The pastor followed up with, "Let's have a prayer honoring the death of the marriage." The husband said it was beautiful! *Beautiful?!* Why wouldn't the pastor say something like, "No, it's wrong, and it can be made better. No, this evil." If we won't, who will?

And the Church goes on, at worst as if nothing really happened, and at best with offering love and support to both parties. But it has not said, "This is wrong, and there are consequences to this wrongness." Why? Why have we bought the bill of goods sold to us by this post-marital culture? Why have we lost our bearings? One primary answer is this: We no longer see ourselves as theological men and women, but rather therapeutic men and women. We have lost our moral bearings and a moral sense of the universe with ourselves as moral actors. We have turned to a God whom we can love rather than one we can obey. We have an infatuation with the love of God but are embarrassed at His holiness.

The Primary Lesson of the Divorce Culture

The primary lesson learned by adults and children of divorce is this: *Love is not reliable.* Its corollary is that the family is not a person's most important commitment. The divorce culture teaches what you want is more important than what is good for the people you are supposed to love and even the people for whom you are responsible. When parents demonstrate to their children that the family is not the most important thing, but that individual desires are more important than solemn commitments that form families, the family loses its power to hold together its members.

Sadly, as divorce becomes more the rule than the exception, stigmas against it inevitably whither away. It becomes increasingly difficult to stigmatize a majority practice. Unwilling to pass judgment or risk breaches with their friends and siblings, people no longer say that divorce is bad, even for the children. Instead, they congratulate one another on having the courage to create a new life for themselves and their children.

As a result, we are giving license to this divorce culture. I believe this is the situation we currently face in our country and our churches. We may not agree with the prevalence of divorce, and we may not believe that couples should separate, but by using their language and throwing our hands up in the air as if there is nothing we can do, we become complicit in their lies.

Relationships Really Do Matter

We need to regain an understanding of "relationship" as central to our understanding of marriage and family. Most individuals desire to break out of our isolation and loneliness and enter into a relationship that offers a sense of home, an experience of belonging, a feeling of safety, and a sense of being well connected. But every time we explore these relationships, we discover quickly the difficulty of being close to anybody and the complexity of intimacy between people. The stronger our expectation that another human being will fulfill our deepest desires, the greater our pain when confronted with the limitations of human relationships.

What does it mean to love another person? Mutual affection, intellectual compatibility, sexual attraction, shared ideals, and a common financial, cultural, and religious background can be important factors for a good relationship, but they do not guarantee love.

I once met a young couple who wanted to get married. Both were attractive, intelligent, had similar family backgrounds, and they were very much in love. They had spent many hours with qualified psychotherapists to explore their psychological pasts and face their emotional strengths and weaknesses. In every respect they seemed well prepared to get married and have a happy life together.

Still, the question remains—will these two people be able to love each other not just for a while or a few years, but for a lifetime? They had been together for a long time and felt secure in their love for each other. But would they be able to face a world in which there is little support for a lasting relationship? Where would they get the strength to remain faithful to one another in times of conflict, economic pressure, deep grief, illness, and necessary separations? What would it mean for this man and this woman to love one another as husband and wife until death?

Marriage as Vocation

The more I reflect on this, the more I feel that marriage is foremost a vocation—two people called together to fulfill the mission God has given them. Marriage seems like a spiritual reality. That is to say, a man and a woman come together for life, not just because they experience deep love for each other, but because they believe that God loves each of them with an infinite love through the death and resurrection of His Son, Jesus Christ, and has called them to each other as living witnesses of that love.

All human relationships, be they between parents and children, husbands and wives, friends, or members of a community, are meant to be signs of God's love for humanity as a whole and each person in particular. While the unbeliever may know how to show love for family, friends, or children, this love is even greater for the believer in Jesus Christ who has the very power of God at his disposal. This is an uncommon viewpoint, but it is the viewpoint of Scripture. Jesus says, "A new commandment I give to you, that you love one another: just as I have loved you, you also are to love one another. By this all people will know that you are My disciples, if you have love for one another" (John 13:34–35). How does Jesus love us? He says: "As the Father has loved Me, so have I loved you" (John 15:9). Jesus' love for us is the full expression of God's love for us, because Jesus and the Father are one (John 14:10–11).

At first these words may sound unreal and mystifying, but they have a direct and radical implication for how we live our relationships on a day-to-day basis.

Jesus reveals to us that we are called by God to be living witnesses of His love. We become such witnesses by following Jesus and loving one another as He loves us. What does this say about Christian marriage and the Christian family? It says that the source of the love that sustains it is not the partners themselves but God who calls the partners together. Loving one another is not clinging to one another in order to be safe in a hostile world, but living together in such a way that everyone recognizes us as people who make God's love visible to the world. Not only does all fatherhood and motherhood come from God, but also all friendship, partnership in marriage, and true intimacy and community. When we live as if our relationships are "human-made" and therefore subject to the shifting and changing of human regulations and customs, we cannot expect anything but the immense fragmentation and alienation that characterize our society. But when we understand God as the source of all love, we discover love as God's gift to His people.

Making a Great Marriage and Family

Paul says in his Letter to the church at Ephesus, " 'Therefore a man shall leave his father and mother and hold fast to his wife, and the two shall become one flesh.' This mystery is profound, and I am saying that it refers to Christ and the church" (Ephesians 5:31–32).

I believe the comparison between what occurs in our relationship with God and what occurs in our relationship with our spouse is important. I don't always feel like a Christian, nor do I always think or act like a Christian. Fortunately, my faith is not a matter of my earnest efforts. Faith is a gift, but it is a gift offered through the offices of the Church, the means of grace.

I think we have made a big mistake in implying that our spiritual life, our relationship to God, is mostly a matter of what feelings we manage to muster. My relationship to Christ is also a matter of keeping at it, of habits, of persisting in the disciplines of faith. Feelings are fine, as far as they go. But feelings are notoriously short-lived. Habits keep us close to God even when feelings are not there.

You show me a marriage based only on feelings, and I'll show you a short-lived affair. Most of us find that the love of marriage needs ritual, habit, and discipline to keep love in marriage. If the relationship is to grow, a marriage must develop and nourish opportunities to be together, to talk, to make love, to have fun, to hang out doing nothing, to work and serve together in activities outside the marriage.

Holding Marriages Together: How Do We Do That?

The Church needs to take a stand on marriage beginning where the Scriptures begin, where the prophets of old began. The Church lives at the intersection of cultures, between a culture of divorce and a culture of permanence. Most Christians speak conflicting languages when trying to articulate what they believe. Divorce is only one prominent issue; the same could potentially be said about any other matter that may be gathered under the title "family values." The Church's task is not to draw up an eternal list of family dos and don'ts and then congratulate itself for being a champion of family values. Rather, the questions that the Church should be asking are these:

> * *What must we say to bear witness against shallow and false understandings of marriage in our culture, just as Jesus and Paul bore witness against shallow and false understandings of marriage in theirs?*

> * *What must we say and do to form our communities so that they bear witness to God's creative intent for permanent, one-flesh union of man and woman in Christ?*

When these become the framing questions for our daily discourse, we will find creative ways to make the New Testament's witness against divorce speak to our time, just as the New Testament writers found creative ways to make Jesus' teaching against divorce speak to theirs.

The question, in other words, is not what family values we should hold, but what kind of Church we should be in order to witness to the truth of the Gospel. The Church's participation in cultural debates about family values cannot take precedence over this far more fundamental matter. We must learn to discern the extent to which cultural narratives captivate our moral vision and determine to engage in the reconstructive work of ordering our language and behavior to the horizon of the biblical narrative. The language of family values has become too politicized to be serviceable in this regard. I submit that what the Church needs instead is to go back to the very beginning, like Jesus, and discuss and hold up a grand picture of what marriage was designed to be.

A key to regaining a healthy understanding of marriage is to take people back to the Word of God and what marriage means. It is important to help people understand old-fashioned words, like *duty, honor,* and *fidelity.* In Matthew 19, in a debate with the Pharisees, Jesus does not want to talk about divorce—He wants to talk marriage. So He takes them all the way back to the beginning.

And Pharisees came up to Him and tested Him by asking, "Is it lawful to divorce one's wife for any cause?" He answered, "Have you not read that He who created them from the beginning made them male and female, and said, 'Therefore a man shall leave his father and his mother and hold fast to his wife, and they shall become one flesh'? So they are no longer two but one flesh. What therefore God has joined together, let not man separate." They said to Him, "Why then did Moses command one to give a certificate of divorce and to send her away?" He said to them, "Because of your hardness of heart Moses allowed you to divorce your wives, but from the beginning it was not so. And I say to you: whoever divorces his wife, except for sexual immorality, and marries another, commits adultery." (Matthew 19:3–9)

Faithfulness and fidelity are no longer terms held in high regard. Fidelity goes beyond a loose understood of simply not having affairs. It is actually a more complex bundle of ideas. The wedding vow holds many promises. When we married, my wife and I promised "to have and to hold from this day forward, for better or for worse, for richer and for poorer, in sickness and in health, to love and to cherish, until death parts us." This is far more than a promise not to cheat. It is a promise to stay, to care, to treat with a most profound affection, to love and to cherish. At its core lies a central notion of integrity—*keeping your word.*

In ordinary language, infidelity—literally a lack of faithfulness—refers to adultery. In the context of the marriage vow, it plainly refers to a breach of any one of these promises. We frequently miss this. A husband says to his wife, "I am leaving you because I no longer love you, but I want you to know that I have never been unfaithful to you." What a self-serving lie! The husband means that he has not had any sexual involvement outside of marriage. But his choice to cease acting with love toward his wife is a choice for infidelity. The choice to leave the marriage altogether is the ultimate act of infidelity.

In a culture that prizes individual feelings over everything else, this notion of fidelity is radically countercultural. A biblical model of marriage and the family places feelings in their proper perspective. Rather than allow feelings to determine behavior, the child of God uses his thoughts and behaviors to elicit his feelings. We must remember that we are as likely to act ourselves into a new way of feeling as to feel ourselves into a new way of acting. Regardless of how I might feel at a particular moment, through faith God enables me to do what is right.

A good marriage is often not so much a matter of choosing carefully as of loving well and stubbornly. According to the Bible, love is something God does. The Bible commands us to view love as a commitment to do for others those things that will help them become what God wants them to be. Matthew 5:44 calls upon us to love our enemies; Luke 10:27, to love our neighbors; and John 13:34–35, to love one another. In Ephesians 5:25, husbands are commanded to love their wives. In each instance, the biblical writers make it clear that love is a commitment to action.

Yet on our own we can never fulfill even one of these calls to love others, let alone our spouse. Only through the faith granted us at our Baptism are we able to begin this process: "God shows His love for us in that while we were still sinners, Christ died for us" (Romans 5:8).

Where Do We Go from Here?

Where do we go from here? The solution is for the Church to once again be faithful to her theological and scriptural foundations. Do you want to make a difference in the divorce culture? Then it is imperative for the Church to serve as a community of moral formation. It must embody the virtues of faith and hope needed to move Christians out of a despairing preoccupation with self. For the Church, the supreme symbol of love is the cross. There, at Calvary, Christ gave up His life for all people.

Where do we go from here? We go to love. Rather, love comes to us. Love is a supernatural gift that is not the sentimental attachments of a man for a woman. It is "labor and fortitude," but in the company of a community of hope—the Church. We may have a natural affection for our spouse, for children, and for friends, and Christian love does not set this aside. But the kind of love that Jesus gives to make marriage a grand and glorious mystery is not natural. It is a gift wrought by the Spirit of Christ Himself. When men and women are freed up from their own self-concern by having their lives and their marriages taken up into the story of God's reign in Christ, they will learn that their marriage and their lives can be, and are, glimpses into the very heart and love of God in Christ. Where do we go from here? Where we always have gone and will go—to the heart of God, to the heart of God broken on a cross for you, for me, for marriages.

Rev. Dr. Bryan Salminen, a licensed marriage and family therapist and a licensed professional counselor, is pastor at Emmanuel Lutheran Church in Cadillac, Michigan. He is the co-founder of Zoe, a Christ-centered, online premarital counseling tool (www.zoescore.com).

Defining Family

BY ROGER SONNENBERG

It is the fifties. Theodore "Beaver" and Wally Cleaver live with their model parents, Ward and June, in their American dream—a tract home. The mishaps of Beaver and Wally are small in comparison to the things we hear about today. Week after week, all of America turns their television sets on to see what is happening to the Cleaver family. Some believe that the Cleavers represent the typical American family.

It is the nineties. Grace comes home unexpectedly to find Will in bed with his new boyfriend. A laugh track accompanies the conversation, slowly desensitizing viewers to the seriousness of the discussion regarding homosexuality. The program has been delighting audiences, gay and straight, for seven seasons. Family is gradually being redefined.

It is the new millennium—2000. The head of the Simpson family, Homer, is not the typical "family man." Though he tries to lead his irreverent family, he finds that the family—especially Bart—leads him. Sarcasm and put-down, vulgarity and rudeness dominate family conversations. Once again, the program is nominated for an Emmy. The values of family are continually challenged.

What Is Family?

Few questions are being asked more than this one: "What is a family?" Even dictionary definitions have changed over the last few years. Traditionally, a family

25

was the fundamental social group in society consisting of two parents and their children. Recently, it has been defined more often as two or more people who share goals and values, who have commitments to one another, and who usually reside in the same dwelling place.

Over the last few years, the courts have considered a much broader definition of family, becoming increasingly inclusive of homosexual relationships and other family structures. For example, because of gay and lesbian formations, we have been forced to revisit our traditional definition of family. Even without the legalization of marriage between gays and lesbians, more and more homosexual couples are opting to have children, once again challenging the traditional definition of family.

The Catholic Church carefully defines family in its Catechism:

> The family is the original cell of social life. It is the natural society in which husband and wife are called to give themselves in love and in the gift of life. Authority, stability and a life of relationships within the family constitute the foundations for freedom, security and fraternity within society. The family is the community in which, from childhood, one can learn moral values, begin to honor God and make good use of freedom. Family life is an initiation into life in society. (Catechism of the Catholic Church 2207, p. 533)

There can be little doubt that Scripture clearly regards the family as the "original cell of social life." Already in Genesis, Adam and Eve provide us with God's design for families. Mary and Joseph were used as the framework in which Jesus grew "in wisdom and stature, and in favor with God and men" (Luke 2:52 NIV).

Though there are different descriptions of families in the Bible, there is no clear definition in the Bible. The closest thing to a word in the Bible defining family would be the Greek word *okkia* (translated "household"). The word described more than just those who were tied together biologically or by marriage; it was used to refer to anyone living in the house, including servants.

Some feel that "family" is too narrowly defined, causing many people within the Church to believe that anything to do with family ministry excludes them. They include the single, the widowed, the unmarried. In reality, everyone is part of a family or has a family. Everyone has a mother and a father, even if they are absent from their lives. The definition of family is not based on marriage. A single person living with his/her mother is a family unit. In some respects, individual churches might be considered families—families united together to support one another. We read of the Early Church, "All the believers were together and had everything in common" (Acts 2:44 NIV).

Living Faithfully within the Context of God's Word

The reality exists that there are many different family structures defined, even in Scripture. Some of the structures are—even at best—dysfunctional. However, God has and continues to work through these different structures. There should be little doubt about this fact when one studies Jesus' family tree. A careful look at it reveals how God used everyone from kings to killers, from priests to prostitutes in order to bring salvation to the world.

An important question in discussing family is to ask whether or not what we call our family matches God's definition. Jesus died to bring us into relationship, not only with God our Father, but also with one another. Jesus blesses us through our relationship with Him. Jesus summarized this truth for us: "'If you hold to My teaching, you are really My disciples. Then you will know the truth, and the truth will set you free'" (John 8:31–32 NIV).

Husband/Wife

From the very beginning, God gave the highest priority to the husband-wife relationship: "A man shall leave his father and his mother and hold fast to his wife, and they shall become one flesh" (Genesis 2:24). This verse certainly contradicts the definition that is becoming more popular in the twenty-first century, a definition that includes same-sex marriages, since it states that God's plan was for *a man* and *a woman* coming together to create a "one flesh" relationship.

Another relationship that has long been popular is cohabitation, where two unmarried people of the opposite sex live together. These couples reason, "We want to try our relationship out to see if it works before we marry!" or "We don't need a license to be married!" This runs contrary to anything Scripture says about family. Marriage is not something you try out, but instead is a lifelong commitment between a man and a woman (Matthew 19:4–6). The commitment of marriage exists to keep people from promiscuous sexual activity. Even in this sinful act, God's Word is always proven correct. Studies have shown that those who live together, and then marry, have a 53 percent higher rate of divorce than those who have not cohabited. They have lower levels of marital interaction and higher levels of disagreement. Though

defining family

many couples cohabitate in order to avoid the stress and expense of a divorce if the relationship doesn't work out, studies show cohabitating couples experience as much if not more stress when they break up than if they had been married. Often there are financial repercussions beyond what these couples would have experienced had they been married—especially for women.

Husband/Wife/Children

In Scripture we see that part of God's design for the family is that a husband and wife procreate and raise their children in God's ways. Adam and Eve serve as our prototype. God's command to them was clear: "Be fruitful and increase in number; fill the earth and subdue it" (Genesis 1:28 NIV).

Another trend in today's society involves having children outside wedlock. One out of three children born today are born to single parents. Though the single parent and child are recognized as a family, such a family structure cannot offer what God desires in a covenant relationship between husband and wife, a father and mother who are both present in the child's life. The training of the child is best done when two parents are present. Throughout Scripture parents are told to teach their children: "Talk about them [God's commandments] when you sit at home and when you walk along the road, when you lie down and when you get up" (Deuteronomy 6:7 NIV). "Fathers, do not provoke your children to anger, but bring them up in the discipline and instruction of the Lord" (Ephesians 6:4). A recent study showed that a father's wrestling with his male child helps the child know his limitations in using his strength in dealing with other people. The healthy interaction between a husband and wife teaches their children how to treat those of the opposite sex.

Contrary to what some would have us believe today, children *are* a blessing from God. Some women's groups try to downplay the importance of childbearing. They suggest that day-care centers can easily replace what any stay-at-home mom can do. God's Word clearly contradicts such thinking.

Because God's design is mother, father, and children, the increasingly popular practice of same-sex couples adopting children ought to be greatly discouraged. Children need, and yearn for, both male and female role models. It is for this reason God put such structure into the world from the very beginning when He created man and woman.

Some married couples cannot have children. Over the years the incidence of infertility has risen, due in part to the growing number of couples who marry later in life. Many of these couples go to great lengths in their attempts to have children.

Still other couples intentionally choose not to have children. The important question is why they choose not to have children. Are their reasons purely self-serving, or are there legitimate reasons for making such a decision?

Certainly God did not design the gift of sex within marriage merely for procreation. God created man and woman with an ability to enjoy sex, to receive pleasure from it. Pleasure was not some afterthought of God's. God illustrates this truth so beautifully in His Word found in the Song of Songs: "All night long on my bed I looked for the one my heart loves" (3:1 NIV).

Husband/Wife/Children/Kin

In the movie *My Big Fat Greek Wedding*, it did not take long for the groom-to-be—a non-Greek—to recognize that for his bride-to-be, "family" meant hundreds of aunts, uncles, cousins, nephews, nieces, and so forth. Many Old Testament families were much like this family—large and apt to celebrate special events. Surveys tell us that today's families are smaller and less likely to gather together for celebration. Extended family members often live far apart and have little, if any, contact with one another. For this reason experts tell us that children today, though they are sophisticated and knowledgeable about many things, are not mature. Why? In order to have maturity they must have regular contact with other adults. Adults help them organize and make sense of the knowledge they have. However, children today have little contact with adults, other than their own parents and teachers. Extended family members, such as grandparents, are no longer around to offer guidance and direction and thus they lack maturity. Aunts and uncles live far away and often have no meaningful relationship with children.

Adam and Eve once again serve as our prototype for extended kin relationships. The importance of kin and relationship with blood relatives is seen in phrases such as "bone of my bones and flesh of my flesh" (Genesis 2:23 NIV). References to such blood attachments seem to validate the importance of extended family (Genesis 29:14; 2 Samuel 5:1). Though Scripture is clear that a husband and wife are to "leave . . . father and mother and be united"; it also says that we are to "honor . . . father and mother" (Genesis 2:24; Ephesians 6:2). As Martin Luther says in the explanation of the Fourth Commandment, "We should fear and love God so that we do not despise or anger our parents and other authorities, but honor them, serve and obey them, love and cherish them." The importance of brotherly love is seen in such verses as Proverbs 18:24: "There is a friend who sticks closer than a brother" (NIV).

Though God's original design may have included husband-wife relationships along with children and extended family, this is not to say that God cannot and does not use other structures to carry out His divine purposes. Scripture clearly demonstrates how in stories such as Ruth and her mother-in-law, Naomi (the Book of Ruth), and in single-parent homes (2 Kings 4:1–7), God did His work.

The important thing to remember is that Christianity is about relationships—relationships made possible through the life, death, and resurrection of Jesus. Healthy relationships are possible because of the vertical relationship between us and God. Because of our relationship with God through faith in Jesus Christ, those relationships known as horizontal relationships are possible. Romans 1:18–32 defines what happens when people become godless and are no longer attached to God through faith. "For although they knew God, they neither glorified Him as God nor gave thanks to Him, but their thinking became futile and their foolish hearts were darkened" (Romans 1:21 NIV). Confused about their relationship with their Creator, the people became confused and skewed in their relationship with others.

defining family

God loves people, all people. Through Jesus Christ, God's family includes those who are biologically nuclear families, stepfamilies, single-parent families, and grandparent-headed families. His family consists of the widowed, the never-married, and the man/woman who struggles with his/her sexuality. He loved the world and all people enough to send His Son, Jesus, to die for them so that we might be united together as family—now and in eternity.

Considering the discussion above, what do you think?

1. What are some of the family structures described by these verses in Scripture?
   Genesis 2:24

   Deuteronomy 21:15

   Ruth 1:8, 14–15

   2 Kings 4:1–7

   Genesis 15:2–3

   Luke 18:15–16

   Acts 4:32

   Which of these structures do you think were favorable in God's eyes? Nevertheless, how did God work through these families?

2. In your observation of families, perhaps your own, how is a family's health determined by the health of the relationship it has with God?

3. What forces from the outside (i.e., television, Internet) are creating and altering new family structures? Why?

Families Color Who We Are

Families have the most profound of all influences on who we are and what we do. They color the details of how we think, what we say, how we act. They determine what we do and how we do it. The role they play may be hurtful, and at other times helpful. They can bring us sadness, but more often they bring us joy and purpose. They shape us from birth to death.

Studies have recently shown that "family" for the majority of people is more important than anything else in life. It is more important than recreation, status, or career. Every person is intricately shaped by his or her family.

St. Paul colors in the picture of how families look in Ephesians 5:22–6:4. He uses the colors of "love" and "respect" to describe husbands and wives. He speaks of honoring one another and not exasperating one's children as distinguishing characteristics of the people of God.

No institution, no group of people, can better minister to the family than the Church, because the Church has the truth of God's Word. The Church alone has the coloring crayons of God's Word. It is the Word that shows Jesus, "the way and the truth and the life" (John 14:6 NIV). In the Word Christ proclaims that He offers "life . . . to the full" (John 10:10 NIV).

Considering the discussion above, what do you think?

1. In what way has your family shaped you?

2. In what way might we look at others and treat them differently if we believed that people are, in large part, what their families and environment made them?

3. Why is instruction in God's Word so essential for coloring the family?

Family Ministry

One of the newest rostered positions in The Lutheran Church—Missouri Synod is that of "Family Minister." Family ministers are those who intentionally conduct ministry to families. This ministry includes more than caring for parents with children or married couples. It involves everyone in the congregation.

Studies tell us that one of the most pressing needs among unchurched people is the need for an "anchor." Many of the promises made by the so-called life experts haven't worked. The anchors they've provided prove unreliable. They gave way and sent too many drifting into uncharted and stormy waters. Truth is elusive.

Family ministry provides one way to bring truth to the unchurched as well as the churched. It supplies the anchor in the person of Jesus Christ. Though many of the unchurched may never poke their heads into a worship service, they might come for a parenting class. Unchurched parents who don't know what do with their daughter who has run away two times or the man who struggles with his marriage may consider going to a special parenting program at the church for the sake of their children, if no one else.

Jesus demonstrated over and over again what His Word can do in people's lives. Consider the story of the wedding at Cana. Jesus performed a miracle to demonstrate His glory. The result was that "His disciples put their faith in Him" (John 2:11 NIV). Jesus continues to perform miracles in the lives of people through Word and Sacrament. He continues to mend relationships between parents and children. He heals the guilt of divorce.

Every family ministry program must begin with a mission statement. Develop this statement after taking a survey of the congregation and establishing a family life

defining family

task force. One congregation adopted the following mission statement: "To share Christ's love with everyone and everywhere." This mission statement directs every aspect of the congregation's ministry, including family ministry. They've defined family as anyone who has, or has had, a mother. That, of course, includes everyone!

Within the task force establish BROAD goals. Broad goals are overarching, extending over a long period of time, such as a year or three years. They are broad, not specific. For example, a broad goal might be "to enrich marriages" or "to support parents." BROAD is an acronym:

B—Big
R—Reaching out
O—Open-ended
A—Attentive to needs
D—Directive

Once these goals are established, put together five to eight specific, or SMART, objectives (desired outcomes) to facilitate each broad goal. These objectives offer strategies on how to achieve the broad goals. An example of smart goal might be to "have a special session outlining the dangers of the Internet in April 2006 with at least twenty youth and parents in attendance and at least four of the participants being unchurched". SMART is also an acronym:

S—Specific
M—Measurable
A—Attainable
R—Reasonable
T—Timely

Every family task force should examine what they offer or could offer in the following three categories:

1. Crisis intervention
2. Transitional ministry
3. Preventative ministry

The Church has traditionally been quite attentive to crises. A couple calls the pastor in the middle of the night informing him that their daughter has just been killed in a car accident and they are at the hospital. More than likely, the pastor goes immediately to the hospital. It is the transitional stuff that the Church often lacks. For example, most churches lack a support group for the family as they go through the grief of losing their daughter.

More often than not, the Church is reactive rather than proactive. Congregations often respond only after something—usually something unpleasant—occurs. From the medical profession we learn that "an ounce of prevention is worth a pound of cure." With preventative ministry we have the opportunity and privilege to prevent a crisis from occurring, such as a divorce or a parenting problem. Marriage enrichment and parenting classes can greatly reduce the chances of a crisis occurring.

Family ministry can be that "ounce of prevention."

    With all probability, the definition of family will continue to be debated over the coming years. Despite the attempt of some to redefine family, God's Word alone directs us in determining not only what a family is, but how to live as a family. One thing is certain: "He who did not spare His own Son, but gave Him up for us all . . . [will] graciously give us all things" (Romans 8:32 NIV).

Considering the discussion above, what do you think?

1. *In what way does the overall ministry of the Church differ from family ministry?*

2. *Of the three aspects of family ministry—crisis intervention, transitional ministry, preventative ministry—which does your congregation do best? Which areas do you need to work on?*

3. *How might family ministry be used to reach the unchurched in your community?*

Rev. Roger Sonnenberg serves as senior pastor of Our Savior Lutheran Church in Arcadia, California.

Getting Started:
A Blueprint for Congregational Family Ministry

BY STEVE AND DEE CHRISTOPHER

Welcome!

Congratulations on your leadership role in family ministry! This is an important role as your congregation responds to the variety of opportunities available to serve families. You have a vital position—be it as a volunteer coordinator, as a professional staff person serving in the area of family ministry, or as a member of a board or committee charged with the responsibility of serving families in your church and in your community. There is great work ahead for you!

Where Do You Start?

Family ministry encompasses a wide variety of possibilities. At first, this can seem overwhelming and cause one to wonder where to begin. Considering the many possibilities can result in a feeling that there is too much to do, which can result in nothing being accomplished. In order to achieve anything worthwhile, it is helpful to have a plan. This chapter is designed to offer help in developing a plan for family ministry in your congregation.

On with the Plan!

Planning can take on all types of detailed steps that look foreboding. We would like to suggest a plan that includes a simple, four-step process. It is designed to consider family ministry from four dimensions organized around the acronym CARE (Concern, Approach, Relate, Effect). Each portion of the plan will be explained in detail. Along the way we'll offer suggestions for reflection, either personally or within a group setting. We hope that through this simple process you gain a basic understanding of each aspect of the design so that you gain insights as you make plans for family ministry in your congregation.

C = Concern

There are a number of concerns that are helpful to consider as you begin the planning process.

The first concern centers on the idea that family ministry is not just another program. The idea of family includes far-reaching concepts when looking at any congregation. Each church encompasses a variety of family units. Just as no two families are alike, no two churches will be the same as they consider how to develop a ministry to families.

Consider some of the family possibilities that exist. You have families with a mom, a dad, and children. You have families with only one parent and children. You find families of three generations living under one roof as a family. There are empty nesters, widows and widowers, singles who have never married, singles who have been married, and those intending to get married. Families come in all shapes, colors, and sizes. Families may look similar, yet each has different needs. In order to address family ministry in a comprehensive manner, you won't want to limit your focus to those in the "mom and dad with children" structure, because there are so many more types of family units that can and should be served.

A second concern is to consider the activities already in place at your congregation that pertain to family ministry. Programs such as Sunday School, youth ministry, and confirmation, to name a few, fit this definition. Family ministry includes what a congregation does to serve families as a unit, as well as individual members of a family. How do you create the new without hurting the existing? How do you eliminate some things without offending? These valid concerns need to be addressed as you plan family ministry in your congregation.

Another concern for many congregations involves the presence of a Lutheran Day School or preschool. There are over 2,200 such schools in The Lutheran Church—Missouri Synod. There are many families connected with these schools, but not with the congregation. They may have their own faith community and church memberships elsewhere in the community. Lutheran schools and preschools are in a strong position to minister to families and to serve them in an important educational manner because of the daily association and regular contact they have with these children and their families.

One great opportunity for service to families involves those children in the school and preschool whose families have no church connections. These families literally exist as a mission field that has come *to* you. It seems natural that churches will want to reach out to these families that have no church home and consider them in developing your family ministry plan.

Another concern is how do you reach out to families who are at various places in their faith development or maturity? Some families have been part of a congregation for generations. Their children know a great deal about the faith and have been raised to be active and committed Christians. There are also families in which faith is a newer experience. They haven't had a long-term church connection. Each type of family has different needs and interests when it comes to growing in the faith. These differences need to be considered in planning a balanced approach to family ministry.

These are just a few concerns that we can identify. There are many others. Some are universal—present in every congregation—while others are unique to certain locations. It is critical that you address the concerns that are most pressing for your congregation as it embraces the challenges of family ministry.

A Time for Reflection

What are your concerns?

What ministries are in place in your church that already serve families in some way?

How are these programs doing? Are they fulfilling their purpose(s)?

What do you need more of in terms of serving families?

What could be happening? What should be happening?

A = Approach

When designing a house or commercial building, even with input from the future owner or tenants, an architect lays out the basic design of the building. Sometimes a team of architects consult with one another. Whatever the process, eventually a design gets on paper, and the discussion gets going. Someone has to make some initial decisions about size and shape of the building, where to locate the doors and windows. The basics are placed in the first draft of the design. In the next stage, the owners or builder react to the design and offer suggestions or changes that make the building more suitable to their needs and desires.

In this next step of planning for family ministry, we would like to suggest a model, a basic design that you, the family ministry leader, can use as a guideline. It is a blueprint, a form you can adjust, tweak, or redesign as you wish. The goal is to make the blueprint fit your congregation and its unique family ministry opportunities.

The approach we suggest to address all of these previously mentioned concerns, as well as the unique issues that face every congregation, involves a family ministry matrix (see example found at the end of this chapter). This matrix approach allows for the connection between existing programs and services to families, for growth and development in new emerging areas of ministry, and for incorporating those future family ministry plans that will be determined at a later time. The matrix is divided into a vertical axis, which represents family stage life events, and the horizontal axis, which describes the congregational ministry connections.

Vertical Axis

The vertical axis represents family stage life events. These are the normal, as well as unique, experiences that take place in the course of the lifespan of an individual within a "traditional" nuclear family. We identify twenty-five such events as shown on the sample matrix. These events are divided into four subcategories: Pre-Family, Children, Youth, and Adults.

We know that there are other events or variations of the ones identified—thus the beauty of the matrix! As you develop your own matrix for your congregation, *you* determine the family stage life events that represent your congregation and community context.

Reflection

What groups or age-specific levels are present in your town or community?

How would you like to address these groupings in your congregation?

Are there any priorities at this particular time?

Are there some groups that are doing fine just as they are?

Who is missing? Is this okay?

Horizontal Axis

The horizontal axis allows for the flexibility to create the kind of ministry connection you desire with each of the age groupings you identified in the vertical axis. Here's where your creativity can shine in a variety of ways!

The first step is to determine what general approaches, what broad areas of ministry, could intercept and connect with the previously identified age groupings from the vertical axis. Our sample suggests the following:

1. **Worship and Public Recognition.** *Worship includes that time in which the family of God gathers to praise their heavenly Father and to connect with one another as children within the Christian family. Worship provides a natural time in which to recognize God at work in the lives of His people in various ways as they continue in their life of faith.*

2. **Church Ministry Activity.** *This column represents the support needed or given to the* Worship and Public Recognition *column. It also represents other ministry endeavors pursued by the congregation in an intentional way to serve the special needs of a particular age grouping.*

3. **Congregational Gift.** *This column indicates a special memento, purchased or created by members of the congregation, to recognize a special occasion in the faith life of a congregational family member.*

4. **Home Follow-up Ministry Activities.** *We believe that true family ministry happens within the home. This column provides an opportunity for the congregation to support the family with resources they can use within the home to further faith development of individual family members. These items allow family ministry to center in the home while being supported by the church. These activities avoid being merely church-centered, as is most often the case.*

5. **Ongoing Programs and Special Events.** *This column represents traditional programming and activities currently seen in many congregations. It also allows for expansion of those church programs in such a way that they fit into the wider goals and plans of family ministry. The focus is not simply more programs for the sake of having more programs, but programming with a purpose and a plan.*

6. **Leadership and Staffing.** *So, who is going to do all this ministry? Even if your call or job description includes directing and coordinating family ministries within your congregation, you can't do it all by yourself, nor should you! This column identifies the volunteers, individuals and groups, as well as other paid staff positions that it will take to address the various components of the family ministry matrix. Training, communication, and resources will be required.*

Reflection

What type of "columns" do you have currently in place at your church?

Where do your current ministries take place? Any apparent patterns?

How are your various ministries led and supported? Volunteers? Paid staff?

What kinds of leadership do you desire in the future?

Ongoing Leadership

This approach to family ministry can get very detailed, even complex, and require a certain amount of monitoring. Notice that there are "blanks" in the matrix, empty lines—places awaiting new ideas and approaches to serving God's people in families. There is still more work to do! Years of opportunity lie ahead for you and your church. Who will do it? How will these great ideas get off the ground?

Your role may be that of full-time staff, part-time paid coordinator, or volunteer. Whatever your role, it is important to have support. We have found it helpful for every church that wants to embark on an intentional family ministry process to have a family ministry team. This is usually composed of interested church members of all ages who meet together on a regular basis. This is not a board to report to on a monthly basis, but a team of people who plan, pray, dream, celebrate, and envision the possibilities of family ministry in your church and community.

Family Ministry Team—Suggested Job Description

Membership:

* A balance of age groupings (teens, young adults, middleagers, and seniors)
* A variety of family ministry representations (single, married with children, empty nesters)
* Staff members who relate to families (pastor, DCE, volunteer coordinator)

Suggested Activities for the Team:

1. Meet on a regular basis for planning and ministry review.
2. Stay in touch with family ministry resources from Christian publishers and maintain a resource center.
3. Pay attention to the family trends within your community.
4. Coordinate budget and financial support for family ministry activities.
5. Pray for the families of your congregation in specific ways.
6. Offer training sessions for those who want to be involved with specific family ministry activities in your congregation.
7. Publicize family ministry and encourage congregation participation in these activities.
8. Seek training and continuing education in the area of family dynamics and family ministry from sources outside your congregation.
9. Identify appropriate electronic resources for families.
10. Recognize and support volunteers and staff who work with your congregational family ministries.

R = Relate

"Just do this!"
"Follow this program."
"Do it OUR way."
"Follow these easy steps, and we guarantee success!"

What dangerous statements! Yet at some point many of us involved in ministry programs and planning activities for congregations, whether paid staff or volunteers, would like to believe that somehow these statements could actually come true. We want an easy fix. We want something that will work immediately.

The danger in creating and sharing a model of ministry of any kind is that readers will attempt to apply it to their situation 100 percent, expecting results of unimagined proportions.

This happens with fund-raising programs and with attendance programs. It can happen with youth ministry programs and Sunday School programs. It can even happen with this family ministry matrix!

As you consider this matrix approach to family ministry, we hope you will adapt it for use in your congregation. We believe this method can work; we have used this approach for nearly six years. However, your congregation is not our congregation. Your community is different from ours. You need to find a way to use this resource to meet the needs, challenges, and opportunities of family ministry in your context. You will have to adapt it for your locale.

Now you try it! Work as an individual or a group. Start with an 11 × 17-inch piece of paper. A large sheet works best so that you have a lot of room to create a matrix for your congregation.

> *Step 1: Use a black marker to create the grid for the desired number of items. Use the reflection questions as a resource for creating your own vertical and horizontal axes to represent the ministry potential in your congregation and in your community.*

> *Step 2: With a blue pen write in the items currently in place at your congregation that relate to family ministry. You may need to research church bulletins, newsletters, and even your constitution to discover everything already in place. Check with your church office for additional information.*

> *Step 3: With a red pen write in those items that you desire to do in the near future. Think about what is needed, what is reasonable, and what can be incorporated in your congregation within the next year or so.*

> *Step 4: With a green pen write in those dreams for the more distant future, items that will take a little longer to get going. These items include visions for new ministries three to five years in the future.*

> *Step 5: Decide who has primary responsibilities for these ministries. What will be done to monitor this process? Who will take responsibility? Will it be staff? Will it include new staff called or contracted for this purpose? How will your pastor be involved? These are crucial questions that need to be answered if this approach is to be implemented.*

E = Effect

What will be the effect of such an approach to family ministry? What expectations can you count on being met if you do family ministry this way? What tangible results will be observed? Will there be anything different from the way you already do things?

These are critical questions! The answers will tell you if you are achieving the mission and purpose of family ministry in your congregation. We suggest five outcomes, or effects, that we hope to see happen as a result of following the matrix:

More Faithful Followers of Christ. *The primary objective focuses on seeing a growth in faith on the part of each individual. Everything that happens in family ministry serves this goal. It is our hope that those using this family ministry matrix will through faith become more strongly connected to our Lord and Savior Jesus Christ.*

Deepening Christian Relationships. *God has placed all Christians into a family called the Church. We have local congregations that function as family units of faith. We have brothers and sisters in Christ with whom we share in this journey called life. Our journey is enhanced as we enjoy life together, support one another, and celebrate our oneness in Christ.*

Maturing Disciples of All Ages. *All too often Christian growth and family programs focus on children, neglecting or even forgetting adults. One can learn and grow at any age, through all stages of life. God's Word connects with people of all ages at all times! It is important for a congregation to be intentional about faith-growth opportunities for God's people, no matter their age.*

Strong Family Partnerships. *Another desired result is that family units— be they traditionally structured, blended, or configured in others ways— grow in their commitment to one another. We also seek to bridge relationships with other family units within the faith community and reach out to families in the local community in order to share our faith in the Lord Jesus Christ.*

Ongoing Vibrant Family Leadership. *It has been said many times that "everything rises and falls with leadership." It is our hope that a strong family ministry program will provide support and strength to family leaders. We also seek to raise up positive models of family leadership for the next generation. As individual families grow in leadership strength, so, too, the family of God grows in leadership ability. Thus they benefit the church as the family of God and strengthen families in the context of the local community.*

Conclusion

This outline is built around CARE, an appropriate word to describe people involved in family ministry. You are involved because you care for families of all shapes, colors, and sizes. You care for families as a unit and as individuals. Care is expressed in formal ways as well as in individual and personalized ways. The care we have for families is a reflection of the care we receive from our Lord Jesus Christ. He cares for us, and thus we are called to care for others.

May this model of ministry, as you use it and adapt it appropriately for your setting, enable you truly to care for families in the name of Jesus.

Dr. Steve Christopher works as director of discipleship at Our Savior Lutheran Church in Livermore, California. Dee Christopher has served the Church in a variety of capacities.

A Blueprint for Family Ministry

Family Stage Life Event	Worship & Public Recognition	Church Ministry Activity	Congregational Gift	Home Follow-up Ministry Activities	Ongoing Programs & Special Events	Leadership & Staffing
Pre-Family						
Engagement	Prayers	4–5 Sessions of Counseling	Devotional Booklet/Wedding Planner	Talksheets—Book 1	Engagement Seminar & Luncheon	Pastor: 3 sessions/Family Minister: 1–2 sessions
Marriage	Wedding	Wedding Planning	Wedding Plaque	Talksheets—Book 2	Newlywed Group	Pastor/Wedding Coordinator
Children						
Prenatal	Prayers	Home Visit	CPH Child Kit	Personal Devotions	Mentor Mother Meetings	Volunteer Mentor Mothers
Birth	Baptism	Hospital Visit & Blessing/Baptism Planning Session	FaithChest	Mommy Memory Book	Meals for New Parents	Pastor: Hospital Visit/Volunteers for Meals
1st Birthday	Prayers & Altar Blessing		Bible Storybook	Celebration Home Prayer for First Birthday	Sunday Nursery & Babysitting Corps	Nursery Ministry Team/Teen Babysitters
2nd Baptismal Birthday	Prayers & Altar Blessing		Prayer Pillow	Prayer Pillow Instructions		Prayer Pillow Seamstress
3rd Birthday	Sunday School Dedication	Home Visit & Invitation to Sunday School	Family Devotion Book	Family Devotion Outline	Sunday School/Vacation Bible School	Sunday School Home Visitor Team
Starting Kindergarten	Prayers & Altar Blessing		Photo Frame with Date & Prayer	Send-off Prayer for First Day	Sunday School/Vacation Bible School	
1st Grade & Learning to Read	Bible Dedication		Children's Bible with Note from Pastor & Parents	Bible Reading Program Outline	Sunday School/Vacation Bible School	Pastor: Message in Bible/Bible Organizing Team
Grades 2–3	Children's Message		Bible Video Each Year			
Youth						
Grades 4–6		Home Visit	Family Devotion Book	Outline for Family Devotions & Service Projects	4–6 Grades Youth Group	Parent Ministry Team/Family Ministers
Grades 7–8	Confirmation	Home Visit in 7th/Banquet in 8th/Home Visit & Invite to High School Group	Catechism in 7th/Cross in 8th	Prayer for a Confirmation Celebration	Confirmation Instruction Program; Jr. High Ministry Program	Pastor, Family Ministers, Confirmation Team; Jr. High Ministry Team

Youth

Event						
Grades 9–12	Driver's License Prayer/Blessing	Home Visit by Older Youth	Dog Tag or Special Bracelet, Sunglasses		Programs of Study, Service & Social Interaction	High School Ministry Team
High School Graduation & College Send-off	Prayer & Altar Blessing	Newsletter/Pen Pals/E-Pals	Quilt/Care Packages	Prayer for a College Send-off	Newsletter, Pen Pals, E-Pals	Quiltmakers

Adults

Event						
New Home	Public Prayer	House Blessing Service	Clock			Pastor & Hospitality Team
New Member/Transfer	Reception of New Member	Orientation/Pastor's Class	Coffee Mug	Sponsor Follow-up Dinner	Assimilation Program/New Member Luncheon	Assimilation Team/Volunteer Sponsors
Men	Father's Day Prayer	Mentor Connections			Weekly Morning Bible Study/Retreat/Servant Events/CC	Pastor/Study Leader/Planning Team
Women	Mother's Day Prayer	Special Friends			Yearly Retreat/ChristCare/Home Bible Study	Planning Team/Volunteer Leaders
Singles					Special Events/ChristCare	Planning Teams
Special Needs		Counseling & Support Group			Support/Nurture Groups	Group Leaders
New Job	Public Prayer					Pastor
Couples	Anniversary Prayers	Marriage Vow Renewals			Marriage Encounter/Parent Seminars/CC	Encounter Leaders/Seminar Leaders
Grandparenthood	Prayers of Thanksgiving		Photo Brag Book	Planning Books	Retirement Planning	Consultants
Senior Members	Retirement Prayer	Home Visits			Weekly LifeLight/CC/Trips/Service Groups	Group Leaders/Coordinators
Death	Funeral/All Saints' Sunday	Counseling	Picture Frame	Grief Support Literature	Funeral Lunch/Dinner/Grief Follow-up Visits	Pastor/Volunteers/Stephen Ministers

relationships

5

Relationships:
Dealing with Marriage and Each Person's Role in the Family

BY JOHN W. OBERDECK

At Christmas our daughter Debbie surprised me with a book, *A Father's Legacy: Your Life Story in Your Own Words.* The book filled with blank pages, a dozen per month, with each page containing a question about my childhood. What kind of questions? "Tell me about your mother's cooking. Can you recall your favorite meal?" "When you were growing up, did you have any animals? What were their names?" "Did you pray as a young boy? If so, can you remember a specific prayer? Who taught you to pray?" When I've answered all these questions, a picture of the place I held in my family as I grew up will be quite clear. Debbie included the following explanation for her gift.

Dad,

I found this book and thought it would be of sentimental value in the future. I hesitated giving it to you now because I didn't want you to think that I thought you were dying. I'm interested in your answers to many of the questions to get to know you a little better, since I didn't really know your parents very well. I wanted to explain so that you didn't take it in the wrong way.

Love always,
Debbie

There's more going on here than just curiosity. Debbie's life has been filled with truly significant changes. Within thirty-six months, her mother completed chemotherapy, her parents moved 350 miles north, her paternal grandfather died, she graduated from college and began a nursing career, her maternal grandfather died, her paternal grandmother died, she changed nursing positions, and she changed her last name from Oberdeck to Stamm. Now in the first few months of marriage, she wants to know more about her parents. What shaped and formed them as they grew up? How did they build a family? How were they able to sustain their relationship over the long haul?

Why ask such questions now? These questions are important because the honeymoon high must gradually give way to rugged routine. The process usually happens at the unconscious level. Like a team of sculptors, she and Owen are together shaping what is to become their marriage, chipping away the outcroppings and polishing the rough spots. What they may not yet comprehend is the lifelong nature of this work or the elasticity required for the relationship they chisel. It's not quite marble, but it's not Silly Putty, either. One rough spot is carefully polished, only to have another spot suffer severe weathering. What kind of a place will their marriage be?

This chapter will focus on how the mystery of the marriage relationship provides each partner, as well as each child in a family, with "place." The word *place* has often had negative connotations, as when someone says, "Doesn't he know his place?" or "She should stay in her place." Let me suggest that there's another way we can understand the word without making it a slur or a put-down.

We can look at family as the God-ordained institution that provides us with place. It consists of a safe environment where we can grow, relationships that teach us who we are, and responsibilities that give us purpose and meaning. This is what Debbie's gift is all about. She wants to find her place, as well as the place of her husband, in the marriage relationship. By knowing more about her parents, how they established a safe place to grow, how their love for each other shaped their identities, and how their responsibilities have made life meaningful, she hopes to be better equipped for the mutual task of sculpting the malleable features of marriage. Understanding the concept of place, comprised of environment, relationships, and responsibilities, is a useful model for family ministry within our congregations. Let's explore the possibilities, first by defining terms more thoroughly, and then by applying the concepts to congregation functions.

Marriage and Family Relationships—Providing a Safe Place

The Christian marriage relationship is comprised of sinful people. This fact in itself makes providing a safe place an essential, but difficult, task. Christian husbands and wives learn how to forgive and how to be forgiven. If their relationship is to last, they become adept in saying those difficult words "I'm sorry, please forgive me," and "I forgive you." They grasp two different roles for the benefit of each other—the role of the penitent who confesses and the role of the confessor who hears and forgives.

The tricky part in assuming these roles is twofold. For the spouse who has offended, as all spouses will sooner or later, the confession needs to be genuine, otherwise the "I'm sorry" is nothing more than an attempt to manipulate, hide, and deceive. We know how great the temptation is to cover ourselves, as modeled by our first parents in the garden (Genesis 3:7–8). True confession, however, leaves us without even a fig leaf in self-defense. In saying "I sinned against you," we are totally exposed. We are at the mercy of the other, and we can't underestimate our hesitancy to be totally open spiritually before the one with whom we are totally open physically.

The other risky role belongs to the confessor, the spouse whose task is to hear what one doesn't want to hear, say "I forgive" to what one by nature would never absolve, and then to forget what could be so useful in the future. Just as the confession is to be genuine, so also saying "I forgive you" must be from the heart. Does "forgetting" mean selective amnesia? No, but it does mean we refuse to let the past sins control the present relationship. We relinquish the power to hold the offense against the offending spouse. Sin's poison is rendered harmless by the antidote of forgiveness and love.

Creating the safe environment also assumes that when conflict erupts, the disagreement has boundaries beyond which the argument will not go. Not long into marriage we discover things about our spouse that either really please or really hurt. Intimacy gives this kind of knowledge. We learn where the weak spots, the deep insecurities, and the unhealed wounds are located. We realize how fragile our loved one is, and we realize that there are things we could do or say that would kill the relationship. The vows said at the wedding include the implicit promise never to use this knowledge to hurt or harm our spouse.

As these skills are practiced in the marriage relationship, being taught by the Holy Spirit, we carve out safe places for ourselves and our spouses. We find ourselves participating in the priesthood of all believers by being priests for each other, and we grow in our own understanding of God's mercy and grace through Jesus Christ on our behalf. In this way husbands and wives are able to "submit to one another out of reverence for Christ" (Ephesians 5:21 NIV).

Marriage and Family Relationships—Forming Who We Are

Marriage shapes and forms who we are. While we certainly have a sense of identity going into marriage, the process of becoming one flesh works on husband and wife to shape and mold them in new and unexpected ways. The adage that becoming one flesh may be a declaration at the wedding but takes a lifetime to become fact is certainly true!

Transformations happen as husband and wife negotiate the roles they will take. There is not simply one role of wife and another role of husband into which each must snugly fit. That was the view of family life in the days of Ward and June Cleaver of *Leave It to Beaver* fame. Their household matched the prevailing perspective on family at that time. The family had fixed unalterable roles; the male filling the "instrumental," or provider, role while the female completed the complementary "expressive," or nurturer, role.

We find reflections of this pattern as Adam and Eve are driven from the Garden in Genesis 3. Adam's focus is on his work; he must till the ground with all its newly grown thistles. Eve's attention is directed to the family; she will experience pain in its creation. Our own lives reflect the effects of the curse in our careers, our hobbies, and our relationships. The only difficulty in the Cleaver family portrait is the word *fixed*. Today's marital relationship requires more flexibility, and with that flexibility comes greater appreciation for the abilities of the spouse. Men are healthier when they develop their expressive side. Women are more fulfilled when they sense their productivity outside the home.

The oneness of the marriage relationship may begin through the amazing mystery of physical union, but oneness deepens as wife and husband learn their unique negotiation system through which they mediate conflicts, provide for the needs of the other, and have their own wants met to an acceptable degree. The marriage partners are changed in the process; they mature with each other. Roles take shape but are always open to change when necessary; so Dad does what he never thought he would do by changing a diaper, and Mom learns how easy it is to operate the snowblower.

Scripture informs us that the roles involve a hierarchy of sorts (Ephesians 5:21–33). But the chain of command is nothing like what exists in government, the military, or a corporation. Headship in marriage means self-giving love, the kind modeled by Jesus Christ's love for the Church, a love willing to sacrifice all for the beloved. The response to *agape* love by the wife is submission, but the submission bears no resemblance to begrudging obedience we might find in a workplace. Subservience doesn't describe it either. Instead, the submission Paul describes in Ephesians mirrors the respect that the Church has for her Lord Jesus. Within this hierarchy the welfare of the wife is the chief objective of the husband, and the wife understands and appreciates her privileged position.

The rose-colored glasses through which marriage has just been described are the glasses of Christian faith. In our day-to-day routines we mess this up, sometimes to an exasperating degree. Being both sinners and saints simultaneously means temptation is never far removed. Husbands put their wants and desires first. Wives manipulate to get their way. Competition builds, and the safe place becomes a dangerous place as each tries to occupy the place given to the other.

The Christian couple recognizes sin's intrusion, however, and recalls their roles of penitent and confessor. "I'm sorry." "I forgive you." These words are spoken often in a Christian marriage, and they are not a sign of failure. They are evidence of the shaping taking place as the Holy Spirit guides a life of growing holiness. Christian couples recognize early in marriage that they are not the model marriage described by Paul. But through the power of the Holy Spirit, they truly are becoming that model marriage. Becoming the one flesh they are declared to be continues until death parts them.

Marriage and Family Relationships—Accepting Our Vocation

Why doesn't this get boring? Perhaps for some it does. The process turns dreadfully dull if we think we've completed defining who we are in relation to our spouse and children—as if the task can ever be finished! Instead, marriage is a lifelong Discovery Channel; nothing stays the same very long. He changes; she changes. The addition of children, if and when that happens, changes everybody. Responsibilities outside the home change. Moves occur. Children grow up. Parents are cared for. Every stage of life butts into the established, negotiated marriage relationship and demands a new contract, a new set of roles, a new understanding of each other.

The vocation of husband and wife is the same for each marriage. Paul writes, "Each one of you also must love his wife as he loves himself, and the wife must respect her husband" (Ephesians 5:33 NIV). The application of vocation of husband and wife is unique to each marriage. Some homes have more clearly defined roles in which husband and wife have specific responsibilities with little overlap. Other homes have considerable flexibility. The important factor in creating place for themselves and their children is the degree to which both husband and wife share the same expectations. Since no couple has identical expectations, we are all given plenty of opportunity for negotiation, exploration, and discovery.

What Makes the Christian Family Place Different?

There are three elements we can emphasize in family ministry that make the place created in the Christian home different from other places. The first is that we affirm our own submission to Jesus Christ as our head and as the head of our marriage relationship. We realize that none of us are kings or queens of our own castle, and the domain that we claim for ourselves in the apartment, condominium, double-wide, suburban ranch, Victorian mansion, Craftsman bungalow, or classic farmhouse doesn't really belong to us. We are not our own. We were bought with a price (1 Corinthians 6:20), and that changes our perspective immeasurably.

Second, we recognize the sinner/saint duality in our lives and in the lives of those we love. We live knowing that God's righteous Law is accusing us daily, "for we daily sin much and surely deserve nothing but punishment" (explanation of the Fifth Petition). Nevertheless, we don't live under the Law's curse because we have been set free by the blood of Jesus Christ shed for us on the cross. We live in the joy of the resurrection. Believing this makes us less judgmental and more understanding in our relationships. Living the Law and the Gospel changes our perspective immeasurably.

Third, the faith we received in our Baptism is strengthened by the community of believers that surround us as we gather around the Supper prepared for us by our Lord. Our marriages and our families, though unique, are not separated from the larger community of believers. While this doesn't give us license to dig into one another's business (Paul warns against busybodies in 1 Timothy 5:13), it does mean that we look after the interests and welfare of one another. We care, and are willing to receive care, for our families and marriages. This is a ministry of love we exercise for one another. It is our place in the family of believers.

Plans for Marriage Ministry

How can congregations support families in the creation of safe places where parents and children can learn their roles and relationships together and come to a meaningful understanding of their responsibilities within the household and within the community of believers? Let's assume as a starting point that the Word of God is being preached and the Sacraments are being administered so that souls are fed and nurtured by the Holy Spirit. Let's also assume that there is an entity within the congregation that has responsibilities for family ministry. Where do we begin in helping couples and families find their place?

Assessing Family Needs

First, a thorough assessment of the congregation's families is needed. What are the life circumstances of our congregation's families? How many family "types" do we have? Brainstorm the multiple categories possible: older couples, widowed living alone, empty nesters, families with teens, families with toddlers, newlyweds, young singles, blended families, single parents, and so on. Does any particular category predominate, or are we an evenly distributed mixture along the life span? How do we demonstrate support for families in our neighborhood who are not members of our congregation?

Next, a thorough assessment of the congregation's present ministry is needed. How have we been spending our resources of time, money, and effort? The programs, events, projects, and special observances of the congregation can be listed, with the intention of noting people who are touched by those efforts, both inside and outside the congregation's membership.

Our objective through this research is to become aware of the broad picture of ministry possibilities and become more intentional in addressing person's needs. Consider making a grid as demonstrated in chapter 4. By locating where our ministry efforts and resources are being channeled, we can discover ministry gaps of which we were unaware. Very few congregations have the resources to cover every need of every age and family type. Most congregations will have gaps. Nevertheless, by analyzing our service to families we can make more informed choices concerning allocation of resources.

relationships

Family Ministry Possibilities

Once a group is identified along with a specific type of congregation function, the brainstorming can begin. Framing the question in terms of place will be helpful. "How can we create a place for . . . ?" or even better, "How can we, working together with . . . mutually create a place?" Ministry possibilities at this point can become overwhelming. We need to be focused in what we do, or we set ourselves up for failure. The more specific our objectives become, the more likely we will accomplish what we set out to do.

Keeping our eyes open to hurts that people experience is always helpful, but we also benefit from keeping our eyes open to the healings that take place. Opportunities to rejoice can be celebrated. Our relationships in our families are filled with stories, and our culture is open to sharing those stories. Support groups, care groups, and Bible study groups are all places where stories of our relationships can be told and wisdom gleaned from these hard-earned experiences can be shared. Within the caring places such groups provide, people are able to express their concerns and doubts and receive the encouragement they need. Hurts are healed in the mutual consolation of the Christian community.

Cautions

As with any endeavor, building a ministry for marriage relationships carries with it warnings. Any group that forms in support of marriage will need to establish boundaries of confidentiality. We may have a place to pour out our hearts in a care group, but we don't want the contents sprayed far and wide beyond the group. The group requires a high level of trust. Likewise, people will always need the freedom to decline participation. People do not grow spiritually or relationally when they are embarrassed or pushed beyond their comfort level. Above all, we remember that people are always at a variety of levels in their life of growing in Christ. Patience and love are hallmarks of any effective ministry for marriage relationships.

Concluding Thoughts

I'm trying to keep up my writing in the book our daughter gave me. I want to support her with all the love I can as she and her husband create the place that will be their home and, if the Lord so blesses, the home of their children. Sad to say, I've fallen behind, in part because our own nest hasn't remained empty very long. My mother-in-law, widowed a year and a half ago, has recently moved in with us. We have been busy painting and moving, making a place for her. The guest room has been renamed, because we don't want her to feel like a guest. This is now her home, where she has place.

This is how it should be in our families and in the family of the Church. God allows us to call him "Father" for a reason, because this way we know Him in a relationship we can understand and a relationship that lets us know how we fit in. And fit in we do because we have a place. In the household of God, our place is permanent and well-prepared by our Lord, who told us, "I am going there to prepare a place for you" (John 14:2 NIV).

Rev. Dr. John W. Oberdeck serves as associate professor of theology at Concordia University Wisconsin in Mequon.

Bibliography

Eyer, Richard C. *They Will See His Face: Worship and Healing.* St. Louis: Concordia, 2002.

Gangel, Kenneth O., and James C. Wilhoit. *The Christian Educator's Handbook on Family Life Education.* Grand Rapids: Baker, 1996.

Garland, Diana R. *Sacred Stories of Ordinary Families: Living the Faith in Daily Life.* San Francisco: Jossey-Bass, 2003.

Strommen, Merton P. and Richard A. Hardel. *Passing On the Faith: A Radical New Model for Youth and Family Ministry.* Winona, MN: St. Mary's Press, 2000.

Wright, Wendy. *Seasons of a Family's Life: Cultivating the Contemplative Spirit at Home.* San Francisco: Jossey-Bass, 2003.

relationship questions

1. Changes happen throughout our lives, not just when we start out in marriage. Think about the changes that have happened in your own life over the last several years. Were they earth-shattering or mild? What spiritual resources assisted you as you went through the highs and lows? How did your community of faith support you?

If you felt something was lacking in support from your congregation, make note of it. Brainstorm how that omission could have been filled. Are any people in similar circumstances today?

2. Wives and husbands exercise the priesthood of all believers when they say they are sorry and when they forgive each other. Does this also apply to their role as parents when children are present? Can parents ever be in the role of penitent and the child in the role of confessor?

Private confession and absolution with the pastor is a powerful form of the means of grace because in it forgiveness is announced specifically to the individual. Could family ministry in the congregation engage in teaching private confession and absolution? How might we accomplish this?

3. The home is to be a place of safety, not only physical safety, but emotional safety as well. Yet we know all too well how frequently homes become places of physical and emotional abuse. Family ministry in congregations ought also to be aware of these situations and have means to assist the abused. Does your congregation know of available community resources? What referral procedures are there?

4. Roles within marriage today are much more flexible than in previous generations. This often puts people in unexpected places where they need extra support. For example, many congregations support "mothers day out" programs for mothers who aren't able to get out of the house. What about fathers who find themselves the primary caregivers for their young children? Is there a family ministry opportunity in your congregation for training in managing the expressive and instrumental roles?

5. Use a grid similar to the one on pages 42–43. Begin by listing the different types of family relationships. How many does your congregation have? What kind of "places" are there for these families? Are there gaps for any family type?

Now compare your congregation family types with the family types found in the surrounding community. How similar or dissimilar are they? Does this type of analysis provide ideas for ways for congregational outreach in support of family relationships?

6. We want to be helpful and supportive to all families in our community. At the same time, we realize that the commission of the Church goes beyond simply providing help. As we establish ministries for families, sharing the love of Jesus Christ remains the primary objective. Can we build safeguards in our service to families that will assist us in keeping Jesus Christ the center of our work?

Touchpoints:
Identifying Opportunities to Minister with Families

BY CRAIG S. OLDENBURG

Three Initial Steps

Let me start out with one of my heartaches. There are too many stories to tell of young adults who were raised by dynamic parents. The parents have been actively involved in key leadership roles within the church, and still the young adults have left their faith behind.

On a recent trip I asked the young woman in the seat next to me what she was reading. After sharing a little about the significance of her book, the rest of the flight was spent exploring the faith she had left behind and the faith she now considered to be the most representative of her world today. She showed no hesitation in sharing and did not seem offended by my interjections. She was open to the faith conversation but very separated from the faith of her family upbringing. Her parents had been active church leaders during her formative years.

The foundation for identifying opportunities to be in ministry with families needs to begin with our own family. The very act of leadership demands we live our message. I recommend looking at (1) who you are, (2) how you stand, and (3) what your territory is before you begin to identify opportunities for ministry.

Step 1: Who You Are

Leaders need to be aware of themselves—of who they are—before they can be

53

reviewing curriculum

aware of others' needs. Are you a lay leader? a pastor? a youth director ? a family life minister? What life experiences have helped you to see who you are, how you react, and how you plan for the future?

Explore your own identity, and most likely you will find you have allowed yourself to be defined by what you do. Instead of our selves defining what we do, instead of our vocation defining our occupation, our occupation defines our very personhood. In all reality, however, how we perform in any occupation is an extension of our self. Who we are drives the life and the ministry that we do.

So who am I? The root answer to this question contains information about family. Family provides the foundation for each of us. It is our roots. We have been shaped by the ingredients of our own family. In discovering opportunities for ministry with families, we can only understand other family systems after we have begun to understand our own. There is no way for us to exist as ministers independent of families. Our core being, as well as the core of those with whom we work, is centered on and influenced by family. As the song says, "We are family."

We are always going to minister with families. There is no way to *not* minister with families.

Fix these words of Mine in your hearts and minds; tie them as symbols on your hands and bind them on your foreheads. Teach them to your children, talking about them when you sit at home and when you walk along the road, when you lie down and when you get up. Write them on the doorframes of your houses and on your gates, so that your days and the days of your children may be many in the land that the LORD swore to give your forefathers, as many as the days that the heavens are above the earth. (Deuteronomy 11:18-21 NIV)

Step 2: How You Stand

My wife and I were having an argument. I don't even remember what it was about (she probably does). I could see it was one of those times of escalation in which a small issue was becoming something it should not be—the symptom of something more serious. We had a carpet style that allowed me to "draw a line" on the floor and I said to her—right in the middle of the argument—"I dare you to cross this line." Now, my wife is no dummy. She knew something was up. She asked, "Why?" I repeatedly dared her. She got more curious. I pointed to the line that was near one side of the dining room table. She circled the entire table, but would not cross the line. I dared her again. She got a stool and put it next to the line and stood on it. By now we were both laughing but still in the argument. I dared her one more time. She finally stepped across the line. I hugged her and said, "Now you are on my team."

It's an old joke, but she understood. We were not on opposing teams. We were on the same team, and the opposition was not us. It was not me against her or above her but with her. I stood with her. Where do you stand?

This second step is important in discovering opportunities for ministry. Open your hand—either one. Now put the word *to* in your hand. Grab it tightly, and with all your might hurl that dirty two-lettered word as far away from you as possible. The closer you keep that word to you in family ministry, the less effective you will be.

What Are We Left With? Opportunities to Minister _____ Families

By now you have probably caught on. Let's put the word *with* in place of *to*. Now you are on the road to an adventure in opportunities. In ministry with families, you have joined their team. You will equip families instead of despairing in the "how to" of modern expectations. Ministry *with* equips families (and the family of Christ) for the job of being in ministry with each other and their community.

All we have done so far in this chapter is to identify the fact that we have no choice but to be involved in our own family ministry and the ministry we do must be *with* families. Both are only acknowledgments of reality. Now we must make a choice. Is family ministry actually ministry or is it mission? Are we in ministry or mission with families? Not that there is really a difference, but for a point of discussion, we need to explore our motivations.

Step 3: What Your Territory Is

I was walking out of a church one day when I caught the pastor in his office. Even though the church is located in a culturally diverse neighborhood, he said their church did not do evangelism. They were not a mission to or with their community. They had a ministry to their members. They were *not* a mission. So, are your final outcomes ministry or mission?

If you are going to be in ministry with families you will need to begin to shed your old "skin" of ministry for an attitude of mission. Mission understands its creed but has no boundaries as to whom it reaches. Mission understands the community as a culture. The families you work with are integrated with the community. Your mission—and the mission of the families you work with—needs to be one of influencing your community.

My friends Bob and Robin work as family life ministers. Their primary ministry is not helping families when a crisis occurs (although they do), but helping families before a crisis occurs. Counselors are trained to work with families in crisis, when life is out of control. Bob and Robin's goal is to build up families so they are stronger than the crisis—before life is out of control. They help families to develop the six family strengths identified by Nick Stinnett and John DeFrain in the mid-seventies in their book *Secrets of Strong Families*. Their mission extends beyond the boundaries of their congregation to affect the community.

Ministry with families begins at home, works with others, and is mission oriented. With these three steps covered, it is time to begin our search for opportunities to minister with families.

Identifying Opportunities

The Opportunities of Crisis and Relationship

How well is your congregation prepared to walk with one another through crisis? Unfortunately, many congregations are highly skilled at turning a blind eye to family crisis.

I remember my friend Mark's dad being shunned when people found out he wanted to divorce Mark's mom. I wonder if our congregation prayed earnestly for Mark's dad and for Mark's family. In another instance, I remember when my parents told me that my best friend's dad had been killed in a car accident. I sat in the basement and cried. I don't recall anyone ever mentioning the loss in church. Were we trained as a family to go through this crisis? Well, that was then and this is now. We understand more fully the mission we are in together.

As church leaders, we need to talk openly and to advocate the support of families in crisis. Leaders need to create a culture of relational response that is not timid. In the open conversation of being ready together for each other and for our community, we find our legs to stand on for family ministry.

We need to help families go through crisis well—since they will go through it! No family can avoid times of crisis. This kind of avoidance is actually a suppression of reality. By having already established a relationship, we can work with families to exercise the skills that help them to embrace crisis well. Within the context of crisis and relationship is opportunity for growth and faith development. We welcome crisis for that reason.

I used to do a short workshop called "Creating Crisis." In the workshop I emphasized the need to create a "mini-crisis" for families to work through so that when the real crisis hit they would be prepared. It was a fun workshop in which families could experience the emotions and challenges of crisis in a playful way with other families. Some church professionals did not receive this idea well, saying that families are already in enough crisis and it would not be right to bring them into a workshop setting to work through a made-up crisis. I disagree. The practice of being the body of Christ is an exercise, not a given. Basic training and teaching methods are best learned through modeled experience. Lecturing from pastors in the pulpits, finger-waving frantic parents, and professors stuck to their podiums provide little assistance when crisis strikes. "For God did not give us a spirit of timidity, but a spirit of power, of love and of self-discipline" (2 Timothy 1:7 NIV).

The Opportunities of Building Strengths

Back in the seventies, Nick Stinnett and John DeFrain researched the common strengths healthy families have and identified the following:

1. Commitment

2. Appreciation

3. Communication

4. Time Together

5. Spiritual Wellness

6. Coping Skills

In 1999, Stinnett published updated materials with a scriptural foundation in *Fantastic Families*. The updated version identifies the family strengths this way:

1. Commit to Your Family

2. Express Appreciation and Affection

3. Share Positive Communication

4. Spend Time Together

5. Nurture Spiritual Well-Being

6. Learn to Cope with Stress and Crises

Your opportunity for ministry with families is to build them up in these skills.

When I was first a DCE in the mid-eighties, I was asked to plan family fellowship events. This usually meant getting families together for a summer picnic or a fall "Hallowed Eve" fair. As fun as it was to do these events, families that did not know how to express appreciation or communicate positively with each other either did not come to these events or came and went home frustrated.

Some of you reading this are asking, "How hard can it be to communicate positively?" Or, "We nurture families' spiritual well-being at church all the time, don't we?" Recall the example from the beginning of this chapter. Young adults are growing up and moving out of the church. Leonard Sweet, in *Out of the Question . . . Into the Mystery*, states that twelve to fifteen Christian churches close their doors daily. We have lost vital relationships in the church because we assume families automatically have the strengths and skills they need to handle life. We do not lack the Gospel message, but we have strayed from living it out as an encouraging and teaching community.

As part of my job I was visiting a congregation that had a crisis in their youth ministry area. Church leaders decided that the crisis was really the family's problem. The family had heard the Gospel message of Jesus Christ—now they needed a congregation that lived out this faith message in a way that builds up the body.

Instead of training each other in the skills of family, we have opted to wait until families begin to show their weaknesses. Then the church tries to swoop in and save the day. Why do we as church leaders and professionals work so hard to set our-selves up as "Super Saviors" when that is not our calling? "For it is by grace you have been saved, through faith—and this not from yourselves, it is the gift of God—not by works, so that no one can boast. For we are God's workmanship, created in Christ Jesus to do good works, which God prepared in advance for us to do" (Ephesians 2:8–10 NIV).

We have been called to equip the body for good works. "So it is with you. Since you are eager to have spiritual gifts, try to excel in gifts that build up the church" (1 Corinthians 14:12 NIV).

The Opportunities of Touch and Blessing

I am on a plane back to Portland, Oregon, after a visit with my parents. I reminded them of the paddle they used when I was young and purposefully resistant to their words of instruction. I do not recall them ever using it in anger, but only in corrective teaching. It was a corrective touch. What I remember even more, however, is the first time my father initiated a hug with me. I was a college student. I remember it as a time of approval and love from him. His hands holding me were a time of blessing.

Teach families to get their hands on their children in blessing rather than in reactive anger. In the book *The Blessing*, the concept of how to give a blessing to fami-ly is explored. Included in the discussion are affirming words and physical touch. We need to promote healthy physical touch among families because our world does not model healthy touch. To do this we must remember step 1 (above). Our first method of teaching is modeling healthy touches and blessings with our own family.

For eight years (1992–2000), my wife and I ran Lutheran Valley Retreat, a camp for children, youth, and families in the Colorado Rockies. Anyone coming to camp received a hello hug from me. Everyone got a hug. No favorites were shown. I cannot count the number of times that people came to me years later and told me how important that greeting had been to them and how it changed their life. Some shared this information with tears in their eyes. It was a hug of blessing, of accept-ance, and of commitment.

Now, not everyone liked these hugs—most often because touch had been a neg-ative aspect of their past. I conduct workshops on community building (maybe we should call them playshops). During these workshops, I share a statistic showing how in any general grouping of people, whether within the church or community, more than half of that population has been either sexually or physically abused. Generally there is silence as everyone ponders the possibility that this is true of the group with which they are sitting. I then go on to show how strategic community building should function in order to move from a wide, no-touch, low-risk community to a tight, high-touch, higher-risk community. The blessing takes place as the people begin to be able to touch in supportive ways. A touch can be life transforming, "Then little children were brought to Jesus for Him to place His hands on them and pray for them. But the disciples rebuked those who brought them. Jesus said, 'Let the little children come to Me, and do not hinder them, for the kingdom of heaven belongs to such as these' " (Matthew 19:13–14 NIV).

The Opportunities of the Least Likely

Caution: Some of you may become disturbed with what I am about to write. But I would like you to take this journey with me in order to consider other opportunities for ministry with families.

Luke 10:25–37 contains the well-known parable that has come to be known as the story of the Good Samaritan. Take a look at your Bible. Before the story begins, Jesus is in conversation with a man who wants to serve God. (Biblical scholars will quickly point out that this may have been a trap for Jesus. We will not focus on the trap but on His answers.) Jesus answers the man by saying that he must love the Lord God and love his neighbor as himself. The man asks, "Who is my neighbor?" Then the story begins. The abbreviated version goes something like this:

1. Man on road to Jericho gets beat up.

2. Two men pass him by.

3. A third stops to take care of him.

4. Who was the good neighbor? The Samaritan.

Look closely. Jesus is calling the man to love his neighbor. Who is the neighbor? Jesus says the neighbor is the Samaritan.

The disturbing news—we *are not* the Samaritan.

Usually at this point we preach and teach about how all of us should want to become the Samaritan. We teach our children to behave like the Samaritan. While this is probably the correct interpretation of the text, I would like to suggest there is possibly one more way of looking at this story. If the neighbor in the parable is the Samaritan, then we cannot be the Samaritan. So if we aren't the Samaritan neighbor, who are we? Are we the one lying on the side of the road needing help?

The one we are called by Jesus to love is the neighbor, the Samaritan. How do we love a Samaritan whom we consider to be despicable and untouchable? Are we to accept help from the most despicable and untouchable person?

Let's translate this to our application. We enter into relationship with people who would otherwise be considered those of bad influence. Who are the untouchable families in our circle of influence? Who are the untouchable families outside of our circle? Why are they outside? Have we only been walking down the safe roads, passing by the opportunities to need help from the "untouchables"?

It is appropriate to enter into relationship with those who are not from our family of faith and to accept help from them. I am not talking about them becoming our spiritual guides or religious leaders. What I am talking about is that it is within this action of acceptance that trusting relationships are formed, and it is within

trusting relationships that ministry with families is born. These are families who need to know Jesus Christ in the fullness of His forgiveness through His life, death, and resurrection.

> Now He had to go through Samaria. So He came to a town in Samaria called Sychar, near the plot of ground Jacob had given to his son Joseph. Jacob's well was there, and Jesus, tired as He was from the journey, sat down by the well. It was about the sixth hour. When a Samaritan woman came to draw water, Jesus said to her, "Will you give Me a drink?" (His disciples had gone into the town to buy food.) The Samaritan woman said to Him, "You are a Jew and I am a Samaritan woman. How can You ask me for a drink?" (For Jews do not associate with Samaritans.) (John 4:4–9 NIV)

Conclusion

Recently I flew to meet with a group of families who were seeking some leadership within their church. As a part of this process, I interviewed and talked with parents and youth. First, I met with the parents. Of course, they were the cream of the crop. They had hearts of gold and values of steel. Next, I met with the youth. It took a while to find out where the youth wanted to go in the conversation, but we eventually began to uncover some of their needs. (Putting youth with a stranger in a cold church meeting room is not conducive to this kind of conversation.) Later as groups of people were standing outside, I got to talk with one young woman who loved to write poetry. She allowed me to see some of it. Much of it had dark themes of death and despair compared to her parents' hopes and dreams that I had heard of earlier.

As I flew home, I could not help but wonder what kind of crisis this family may encounter and if, with such differing worldviews, they would be ready. I was wondering if they had the necessary strengths to cope with any crisis that does arise (especially the one on spiritual well-being—or faith in Christ), but also if they would be able to sufficiently equip others for the task of coping. I saw in this family, however, the ability to be near each other, interact with each other, and touch. I wonder if this young woman who is dealing with issues of death and despair (quite outside of my comfort zone) might be one of the least likely that God is preparing for someone to interact with and accept help from in order grow into relationship with Christ.

Are you ready to take the three steps—consider who you are (living ministry within your own family first), how you stand (ministry with others), and what your territory is (mission-oriented ministry)—before you begin to identify opportunities for ministry? Then, to start, consider the opportunities for ministry with families.

DCE Craig S. Oldenburg, currently completing work for his doctorate, is the founder of Experiential Formations, which explores the community's role in practice of faith (www.experientialformations.com).

Bibliography

Goleman, Daniel, Richard E. Boyatzis, and Annie McKee. *Primal Leadership: Realizing the Power of Emotional Intelligence.* Boston: Harvard Business School Press, 2002.

Smalley, Gary, and John T. Trent. *The Gift of the Blessing,* updated and expanded ed. Nashville: T. Nelson Publishers, 1993.

Stinnett, Nick. *Fantastic Families: 6 Proven Steps to Building a Strong Family.* West Monroe, LA.: Howard Publishing Co., 1999.

Stinnett, Nick, and John D. DeFrain. *Secrets of Strong Families.* Boston: Little, Brown, 1985.

Sweet, Leonard I. *Out of the Question—into the Mystery: Getting Lost in the Godlife Relationship.* Colorado Springs: WaterBrook Press, 2004.

touchpoints

Family
Ministry

Identifying Opporunites

Identifying Opportunities to Minister *with* Families

Read Luke 19:1–10.

Jesus ministry to Zacchaeus became ministry with when He allowed Zacchaeus to invite Him into Zacchaeus's home and eat with "sinners" (Zacchaeus's mission).

How can you change the wordings in your congregation's goals so that they change from to ministries to with ministries?

What will happen differently if the new wording you create becomes the culture of the congregation?

To teach the concept of ministry with, Jesus lived it. How might you live the message of ministry within your family, home, or friendships?

How might ministry change in your congregation if you understood that discipleship with families would lead to their ministry with other families in the community?

Read 1 Timothy 3–4. Timothy was instructed by Paul on how to be an effective young leader of the church. Paul encouraged him to live a life "above reproach" (3:2) and to maintain a healthy family.

What qualities of church leaders are mentioned in these verses?

How would ministry change if the main teachings of the church were lived out more than spoken?

If church leaders lived a life above reproach, what kinds of healthy touch events could you live out with other families that would mentor them in healthy touches of blessing?

What family, right now, has the congregation unintentionally marginalized (seen as the least likely for ministry) due to their family situation? (Don't answer that out loud.) Now decide on how to network families with those in the church that need their support.

BASICS

Generations

BY HARRY KRUPSKY

Intergenerational Connections

I was born in 1950. The culture that surrounded my family did life "intergenerationaly." The elderly were honored; children were a blessing from God. Holidays and holy days were family times. Family gatherings meant moms, dads, sisters and brothers, grandparents, uncles and aunts, cousins, friends. Certainly there were families and individuals who did not live an intergenerational lifestyle, but they were the exception rather than the norm.

Today's cultural values have shifted. More and more elderly are seen to be a burden, and children have become economic liabilities. When you piece together the reality of divorce with the high rate of mobility, it is easy to see the isolation of individuals and families disengaged from intergenerational life. As church leaders who envision and plan ministry, it is at least worth asking ourselves this question: Do we treasure (value) life lived in an intergenerational fashion?

As you answer that question, take your thoughts to the next level. Do I value intergenerational life so much that I desire to see intergenerational ministry in and through our church ministry? These two questions are personal. I would encourage you to prayerfully ponder them and honestly answer them. If you are working with a team, reflect on them together.

Anytime that ministry is developed, it is important to consider how that ministry can be used by God's Spirit to carry out the Great Commission, "Then Jesus came to them and said, 'All authority in heaven and on earth has been given to Me. Therefore go and make disciples of all nations, baptizing them in the name of the Father and of the Son and of the Holy Spirit, and teaching them to obey everything I have commanded you. And surely I am with you always, to the very end of the age'" (Matthew 28:18–20 NIV). Through faith we are empowered to live out the Great Command: " 'Love the Lord your God with all your heart and with all your soul and with all your strength and with all your mind'; and, 'Love your neighbor as yourself'" (Luke 10:27 NIV).

The statistic that 80 percent of new members in the local church first came via the invitation of family or friends has not changed over the last twenty-five years of ministry at our church. The initial command of our Lord to "go" is lived out through our relationships. God used the relationship of Naomi and Ruth to touch Ruth's heart. Paul reminded Timothy that God used the intergenerational connection of a grandmother and a mother to work faith in young Timothy: "I have been reminded of your sincere faith, which first lived in your grandmother Lois and in your mother Eunice and, I am persuaded, now lives in you also" (2 Timothy 1:5 NIV). Paul further mentions how the Scriptures had been taught to Timothy from infancy: "From infancy you have known the holy Scriptures, which are able to make you wise for salvation through faith in Christ Jesus" (2 Timothy 3:15). Can you imagine the storytelling for Grandma Naomi and Grandma Rahab to Ruth and Boaz and then to young Obed? Or how Obed told the stories to Jessse, who told them to David. Consider God's Word through the psalmist: "We will not hide them from their children; we will tell the next generation the praiseworthy deeds of the LORD, His power, and the wonders He has done" (Psalm 78:4 NIV).

God's Word creates a picture of telling the great stories of God from one generation to the next, from one family member to the next. It was true in Bible times, and it is still true today, that the Great Commission of "going" and "making" disciples happens best through the intergenerational connection of family.

So how can God use our church with its resources to help the "inviting" and "storytelling" to take place through the people God has given us? Before offering some practical means and methods of ministry, consider the importance that intergenerational life and ministry can play in opening up lives to the means of grace so that people are growing in relationship with Christ and one another. The Genesis account from Adam and Eve to Joseph clearly shows how sin separates man from God and from one another. The story line of Genesis has not changed in the twenty-first century—only the names of individuals and their families have changed.

The Word of God spoken through Moses in Deuteronomy 6:2: "So that you, your children and their children after them may fear the LORD your God as long as you live by keeping all His decrees and commands that I give you, and so that you may enjoy long life" (NIV) will need to be spoken to each generation. Sin still separates us from God and one another. As God continued to start over again and again with His people in Genesis, so in Christ we as God's children are called upon to keep our hearts open and experience new beginnings through God's kind of forgiveness with one another.

All this needs to be shared because more than ever God's people are not committed to their families, their extended families, or their local church. Instead of living out a ministry of reconciliation, "All this is from God, who reconciled us to Himself through Christ and gave us the ministry of reconciliation" (2 Corinthians 5:18 NIV) today's Christians seek what is new and pain free.

Intergenerational ministry moves against the entire cultural current. It challenges us to stay committed and connected as Paul writes in Galatians 6:2, "Bear one another's burdens, and so fulfill the law of Christ," and in Ephesians 4:32, "Be kind to one another, tenderhearted, forgiving one another, as God in Christ forgave you."

Intergenerational ministry is not some cute trend. It is at the core of living out the Christian life with sinful people. It demonstrates commitment to the welfare of others. It is not about pursuing an easy life. It is about being a Christlike servant to those God has called you to love in your family, extended family, community, and church. Naomi's and Rahab's lives were not easy. They committed themselves to God, and through their lives one of the greatest redemption stories of the Bible is told. Redemption, reconciliation, forgiveness, love, and hope are God-breathed and Christ-fulfilled lifestyles.

As the Church declares the great stories of the Bible through teaching/preaching ministry, it describes an intergenerational lifestyle that would be impossible if not for God's mercy and grace experienced in Christ and lived out in our relationships through the Spirit at work in us. Each local congregation is a unique creation of God's Spirit. The resources and giftedness vary from one congregation to the next. Thus, the form intergenerational ministry takes at each church depends on the vision and the resources within that congregation.

A Personal History

Walk with me through my personal history of intergenerational family ministry. See how God's Spirit worked through my heartfelt value of bringing the generations together for God's Spirit to impact lives with the love of Christ and drawing people deeper into relationships with one another. I served as classroom teacher and youth minister at St. Paul Lutheran in Flint, Michigan, from 1971 to 1975. One ministry vision of mine was to bring together parents and children. I did not have the clarity of purpose, but I knew deep in my heart that it was the "right" thing to do. At times we would have our adult and teen Bible classes come together for discussion and sharing. With the youth leadership we sponsored family gatherings, such as a Halloween party for all ages. As I listened and observed, I saw that intergenerational ministry was used by God to build relationships and create special memories of being a Christian young person.

During my years as a teacher and coach at Lutheran High School North in Mount Clemens, Michigan (1975–81), it was evident that the students whose parents "did" life with their teens had an advantage in developing as a disciple of Christ. Attitudes, values, and even achievements were on the side of students who connected with their families. There was something very special when a young athlete had parents and grandparents cheering them on.

In 1981, God graced me to become family life minister at Faith Lutheran Church in Troy, Michigan. A key part of the vision I carried into the ministry was to help bring families together in sharing faith and life. As we envisioned intergenerational gatherings, one key thought that guided us was "Look for times when families would have a natural desire to experience life in a Christian atmosphere." This idea led us to consider the Advent/Christmas season, New Year's Eve, the Lenten/Easter season, summer family gathering times, and Halloween.

A second key thought that guided our planning was "We desired that the Spirit of God would use the events to help individuals grow in relationship with Christ and one another." As resources were identified, events were scheduled and planned. The key resources were, are, and always will be leaders and volunteers to plan and carry out the event.

The first time we conducted an event, I was usually the point person. One of the first intergenerational evenings that took place at Faith was built around the Advent wreath. I needed volunteers to organize the meal, to coordinate the building of the wreaths, to set up and clean up the facility, and to advertise and sign up people for the evening. Seeing what God did among the families and envisioning how He would use the devotional materials in the homes inspired several people to step up to lead the event when asked the following year. Some evenings, such as our New Year's Eve gatherings, never seemed to accomplish our goals, but others, including the pumpkin patch party at Halloween and the Easter fair on the Saturday before Easter, grew into huge events that exceeded our expectations in scope and attendance over a twenty-year period. Rooms in the building were set aside for different craft projects that were fun for the parents (grandparents) and children to do together. With the crafts came sharing parts of the Christian message. Puppetry, chalk art, and dramas were used to convey the Gospel message in large-group settings during the events. We found these intergenerational congregational events to be great opportunities for our members to invite friends and relatives to experience the ministry of our congregation.

After twenty-four years of family ministry, I would still say that the vision of the leaders and the resources of the local church are the two keys in bringing intergenerational ministry to life. Without the vision there will not be the leadership and inspiration. Without the resources (key volunteers) there will not be enough energy to initiate and develop the ministry.

A Congregational Application

Today intergenerational ministry flows out of our three divisions of ministry in our congregation: children, students, and adults. All of our leaders in these divisions value bringing the generations together to open up lives to the means of grace so that God's Spirit can create and nurture faith.

The mission statement of our children's ministry division is "to partner with parents in helping their children learn about Jesus' love and experience Him in their lives." To live out the mission statement they plan special events each year.

Our student ministry is also devoted to doing ministry in the context of family and intergenerational connections. Adults are trained and are known as youth staff. They serve as small-group leaders, table leaders at large-group Bible studies, coordinators of events, and team leaders on short-term mission trips. This past year student ministries developed a family-based confirmation plan. The following are some key thoughts that describe the "purpose" of the new form of ministry:

- *To help parents teach, pray, and grow with their students as they become members of Faith Lutheran Church by studying the Scriptures and the Small Catechism.*

- *To create a confirmation process that integrates the five desires (worship, discipleship, community, outreach, stewardship) into a student's life.*

- *To help build families in Faith Lutheran Church.*

- *To teach the Small Catechism as Martin Luther intended it to be taught.*

- *To see students and parents embark on spiritual journeys together as a family.*

Through our adult ministries, specifically through our men's ministry, several events have proven to be successful in bringing generations together with one another and Christ.

Whether the events are led by the children's, students', or adult ministry leaders, the common thread would be that the leader has in his or her heart a deep conviction that it is God's desire to work through the intergenerational connection to build disciples. Ministry leaders and key volunteers are inspired to dream and plan for the future as they see and hear what God is doing in the lives of those who attend. The event truly becomes God's ministry.

On one father-son campout, a man from our congregation brought along his dad and his son—three generations sharing a tent. God used that weekend to heal the past and propel them into a growing relationship with one another. One grandfather who is the "teacher" of his seventh-grade granddaughter in the confirmation ministry speaks with tears in his eyes concerning the faith sharing that has taken place in his home. Another man has been a small-group leader on confirmation retreats for ten years. Why would he want to spend a weekend with eighth graders for so many years? His answer is that he loves to hear the students speak about what

generations

Basics

God is doing in their lives! After one of the "Extreme Makeover—Family Edition" evenings, one mom wrote this response to the question "How was your family's experience?": "Great! We loved it. This is the first time my husband picked up a Bible and read it to the family. Praise God! Thank you for everything!"

During a devotional time a good number of years ago, these words of Jesus deeply touched my heart, "I am the God of Abraham, and the God of Isaac, and the God of Jacob" (Matthew 22:32). They speak of three generations who are with Jesus in His kingdom. My mind reflected on Grandpa Krupsky, my dad, and myself. Grandpa and Dad were already in heaven. I thanked God for that intergenerational faith and life that had been passed on. Today when I hear the words of Jesus, I add to that picture my children and my grandchildren, generations of faith that, because of Christ's resurrection, even death cannot separate.

May our great God work His works in the hearts of the generations we are privileged to serve. May He give us the vision and the resources to work in and through the generations at this time in history.

Intergenerational Activity Ideas

Bible Exploration

Third graders receive a new Bible and spend three Sunday mornings with their parents learning how to use it. They learn how to find their way around the Bible, locate treasured Scripture verses, and discover why God gave us His Word.

Extreme Makeover

This evening is designed to help families build a home centered on Christ. After enjoying pizza and salad, the families are engaged in activities that help them experience "God talk." For example, each family builds a sandcastle and then examines the words of Jesus in Matthew 7:24–27. Along with the family activities there are music, gifts, and more!

Children's Christmas Extravaganza

The entire building is utilized to involve children and their families in crafts, activities, puppetry, and so forth. The event concludes as all gather to share the Christmas story in the context of worship. This event has been designed to replace the "traditional" children's Christmas program.

Easter Fair

This annual event is a wonderful way for families with children through grade 5 to experience the ultimate sacrifice and victory of our Savior Jesus Christ! There are games, crafts, puppetry, sing-along, chalk art, and more. There is also an Easter journey in the Family Life Center, where participants are escorted through Christ's Passion Week and reminded of the only reason for our celebration: Jesus' victory over sin and death.

Daddy-Daughter Dance

Each February a team of men put together a fun time for dads (even some grandpas) to share an afternoon with their daughters. This year's theme was "Princess for the Day."

Home Plate

We make tickets available for families to attend a Detroit Tigers game. Prior to the game, an infield clinic is held for the children, followed by several players sharing their Christian testimony.

Father-Son Campout

A man from our church who loves to take his sons camping has put together a team of men who share his vision for bringing the generations together in the outdoors for an August campout.

Harry Krupsky serves as minister of family life at Faith Lutheran Church in Troy, Michigan.

generations

Basics

Questions to Consider

1. On a scale of 1–10, how important is intergenerational life in the growing of disciples? Why? _____

1	2	3	4	5	6	7	8	9	10
NOT NEEDED							VERY	INTEGRAL	

2. What are the benefits of intergenerational life? What are the benefits of intergenerational ministry? _____
_____
_____

3. What are the challenges of intergenerational life and ministry?
_____
_____

4. Consider your church. Where is intergenerational life and ministry already taking place? What might be the next steps in growing this form of ministry? _____
_____
_____

Consider the following areas:

WORSHIP _____

DISCIPLESHIP _____

EVANGELISM _____

COMMUNITY _____

SERVING _____

Consider the ministries of these groups:

CHILDREN _____

STUDENTS _____

ADULTS _____

GRANDparenting

BY RICH BIMLER

Keeping the Grand in Grandparenting

Let's start with some definitions: "Grandmas are mothers with frosting!"
"Grandpas are dads with lots of practice!"

Ministry with, to, and by older adults plays a significant and extremely crucial
role in any congregation. As a greater number of adults grow older and older, there
will be more and more grandparents available for ministry to others. And that's great
news! Church leaders, through congregations, need to mobilize this powerful group of
God's saints in order to provide resources and ministry models to involve in joyful
and affirming relationships, all in the name of the healing Christ!

Here are some methods and models for this to happen through you and in
your congregation. As you reflect on these ideas, be ready to stretch your imagination
and creativity to come up with other exciting ministry opportunities! And remember
this sage saying: "You don't stop laughing because you grow old . . . you grow old
because you stop laughing!" Join us for a celebrative experience of seeking new ways
to affirm and involve the grandmothers and grandfathers around us!

71

Activity 1

As a starter, try this: Do a quick interview with some grandparents in your congregation and family. Ask them the following questions, and add others that fit your situation.

1. *What do you enjoy most about your grandchildren?*

2. *What is your favorite activity with them?*

3. *What is your main worry or concern about them?*

4. *What do you think are the three to five best things you can do for them?*

5. *Describe one or more of your grandchildren.*

6. *How would your grandchildren describe you in terms of your gifts, habits, priorities, interests, behavior style, and attitude toward life?*

7. *How would you describe their faith in the Lord?*

8. *How do you share and tell the story of Jesus to your grandchildren?*

9. *What one thing do you want to do with them before you die?*

After you've completed this survey, summarize the findings. What kinds of statements can you make about these results? What do these reactions tell you about what is needed by grandparents to continue to develop positive relationships and keep within "ministry range" of their grandchildren? Use this data to consider specific ways for you and your congregation to respond to the needs and gifts of the grandparents around you.

Activity 2

Gather a group of grandparents and their grandchildren together for a time of fun, food, and fellowship—with lots of other festivities thrown in! After some introductions, pair off the old with the young, and have them talk about topics such as their favorite movies, songs, baseball teams, or school subject.

Play some games together as a group, asking the young and the old for their favorites. Give prizes to everyone!

Do a "family feud" skit with the older against the younger. Ask questions regarding their favorite foods when they were young, historical facts about past presidents, inventions, and how things have changed over the years. Check various Web sites for data on historical facts and traditions.

Share a devotion together, using Scripture, songs (for the older and younger!), and special readings. (Check out *Devotions for the Chronologically Gifted*, CPH, 1999.) And pray together as God's gifted people!

BE-Attitudes for Grandparents! (Adapted from Matthew 5:1–12)

Jesus gave His people the BE-Attitudes in the Gospel of Matthew as He taught and affirmed people of all ages concerning the priorities in life. We are blessed—every one of us! We are blessed—regardless of our age! We are blessed—because of what God has done for us in Christ Jesus!

Congregations have the privilege and pleasure of celebrating the blessings of life by being in "ministry range" of people of all ages. Celebrate every day the blessings of having many opportunities to rub shoulders with little children, teenagers, middle-aged folks, and even the "golden oldies"!

What follows is a list of "BE-Attitudes for Grandparents." Discuss them, add more to the list, and work hard at putting these, and other BE-Attitudes, to work in your home and community. And have fun in the process!

1. BE-There!

So much of ministry happens because we spend time with each other. When we have time to listen, to share, to pray, and to offer help and hope to others, ministry happens because the Lord is already there!

And grandparents do have time to "be there!" Grandparents, so often, serve as the people of God who share their experiences, offer encouragement to others, and act as a quiet and peace-filled source of comfort and hope. Find ways in your congregation to ask older adults to help in the school, to "kid-sit" while parents are busy, to tell their faith stories in classes and homes, to be there in the name of Jesus!

2. BE Joy-Filled!

Older adults have so much to share with others because they've experienced so much joy and sadness in their lives. Allow them to do this! Scripture tells us, "The Lord has done great things for us, and we are filled with joy" (Psalm 126:3 NIV). What a wonderful verse for grandparents. Grandparents have lived through the hurts and hoorays of life and are ready to celebrate their faith in the Lord! Ask them!

Encourage younger people in your family and church to take the time to listen to the joy in grandparents' lives. Just by asking them to share, you are helping older adults live out their joy. Encourage grandparents, individually and in groups, to be intentional about sharing their joy in the Lord. Have children share cartoons and jokes with the grandparents. Have a section in your church newsletter that shares joy-filled stories from older adults. Joy is contagious—pray for an epidemic.

3. BE Thank-Filled!

We proclaim, "O give thanks to the Lord, for He is good!" And isn't it great to have so many grandparents around us who share their thanksgiving through thanksliving. Encourage your congregational leaders to provide many "thanks" opportunities for people of all ages. This can be done through articles in the church papers, by prayer chains, through Bible classes, and by saying, "Thanks, Lord!" as often as possible. Regularly ask grandparents what they are thankful for. Listen closely, celebrate with them, and watch them beam.

grandparenting

4. BE Human!

Grandparents are human—really. Just like you and me. Accept them for who they are—sinful, forgiven human beings, wounded healers with lots of scars and scratches, worries and woes. But always they are saints in the Lord, forgiven by Christ's death and resurrection, marked in their Baptism as children of God.

Let grandparents be human. Celebrate with them, and help them to accept themselves as both sinner and saint. One of the best ways for older adults to show their humanness is to allow them to tell stories of how the Lord has forgiven them and guided them through their many mistakes and foolish actions. Ask grandparents to tell stories of what went wrong in their lives, things they wish they had never done, consequences of some of their past actions. Let them know also that they are forgiven—always—in Christ. Allow young folks around them to learn from their mistakes.

5. BE Forgiving!

Grandparents are "for giving" and also are "forgiving." One of the greatest gifts grandparents can give to family and church members is the gift of forgiveness in Christ Jesus. One grandfather has a card that reads, "Forgiveness is my business!"

Grandparents live out their forgiveness because they know how their life will turn out. They live on "this side" of the resurrection and know eternal life is ours, because of Christ. Help people of all ages to realize that living in forgiveness is a gift from God alone, in Christ. This gift brings health and hope to all people. Have little children learn to ask for forgiveness from their grandparents and provide opportunities and training for grandparents to verbalize to grandchildren that they are forgiven, every day, in the Lord.

6. BE a Model!

Grandparents model what it is to be a person of God! And what they model is not "how to do it right," but rather "how to live forgiven." Grandparents are called to be "Jesus with skin on" to those around them. They are called, not because of their age, but because of the faith that the Lord has given to them to loudly proclaim that they are loved by the Lord always!

There is a button around that simply states, "I was caught doing something right!" Every grandparent should have hundreds of these to give away to children around them. This is what grandparents model—that God has given all people so many gifts to use to help and enable others to be people of God. Help grandparents do "things right" by allowing them to be models in the Lord!

7. BE Focused!

One wise grandma once said, "There are only two rules in life: (1) Don't sweat the small stuff; and (2) Everything is small stuff." How wise that is. That's what it means to be focused.

Grandparents help others to sort out the priorities in life. Churches can provide classes for older adults and younger people to talk about what really matters in life.

Grandparents can give testimonials to the fact that their relationship in the Lord is what life is all about. Give them permission and opportunities to do so. Congregations focused on proclaiming Jesus Christ as Lord and Savior enable people of all ages to focus on the cross and the resurrection in all that they do.

8. BE Humorous!

Most older adults have a great sense of humor—especially if they are given permission to use this gift! Pastor Walt Schoedel of St. Louis classifies older adults into three categories—the "Go Go's," the "Slow Go's," and the "No Go's." Not only is this quite accurate, but it also uses humor to get the point across! It shows that we can laugh at ourselves!

Provide opportunities for grandparents to tell silly stories, jokes, and funny experiences in life. Perhaps you'll hear some stories more than once, but that's okay. Just smile and laugh anyway! Help older adults lighten up and not take themselves so seriously. Let them do the same with those younger people around them! Someone once asked, "Does God have a sense of humor?" The answer: "Sure, He does. He just has a slow audience!"

9. BE an Encourager!

Encourage . . . encourage . . . encourage! These are the three best gifts that grandparents can give to their grandchildren. Older adults who take the time to listen, to smile, to hug, to hold, and to respond gently and lovingly to the little ones around them are God's special gifts to the world.

All congregations need to work hard at encouraging older adults to encourage others. Through conversations, training sessions, sermon illustrations, Sunday School, and Bible classes, older adults can be trained and given opportunities to bring words of comfort, hope, and affirmation to young ones who desperately need it. The "heart" of relationships in the Lord is encouragement. But don't forget that grandparents sometimes need encouragement themselves.

10. BE Yourself!

"What you see is what you get!" is a phrase that is appropriate for all people, but especially for older adults. Many grandparents have finally learned that the Lord loves them just the way they are. No need to play the game "Let's pretend!" anymore. I am who I am—and that's good enough for me because it is good enough for the Lord!

And what powerful witnesses grandparents can be to help younger folks accept themselves for who they are, in Christ Jesus. Being yourself does not mean thinking too highly of yourself because of your age or accomplishments or gifts or wealth. Rather "being yourself" means that our faith assures us that we are loved and blessed and forgiven through faith in Christ Jesus. It is the Lord who gives us worth. Be who you are—baptized children of God. That's good enough for me.

11. BE a Storyteller!

David Walsh says, "Whoever tells the stories owns the culture." How true. Who, or what, is telling the stories in today's culture? Unfortunately, more often than not, our culture is reflected in movies, television, commercials, music, DVDs, rather than in the Church. Perhaps when we grew up, the Church was telling more of the "story" of what life is all about. But now it is the culture of violence, sex, greed, and self-centeredness.

Grandparents, unite. We can, and must, continue to tell the story. And what is our story? It's the story of Jesus and His love for all people. It's the story that grandparents, who have experienced this love through their families and congregations, have lived and taught for years.

The story needs to be told, more strongly and deliberately than ever. Right now—today. Help put older adults and younger people together to learn to tell the story of Christ's love. Provide classes and opportunities for this to happen. Gather people of all ages together, and teach them the basics of our faith. Provide opportunities for them to share the story with others.

12. BE Ready!

Remember the old saying "Get Ready, Get Set . . . Go"? Often it becomes instead "Get Ready, Get Set, Get Set, Get Set" and we never get to GO! Grandparents are in a marvelous position to help others get ready for life and then help others move to "Go" in the name of the Lord.

Older adults have been practicing for many years to "get ready" for life. Now it is their time to help others to "get ready." They do this by teaching others, through word and action, what it means to be "ready" for life in Christ. They begin with their Baptism and move on by knowing whose they are! Bring people together to renew their baptismal promises. Provide classes, informally and formally, for the old and the young to grow through the Scriptures. Provide mission trips, work camps, and retreats so that old and young can rub ministry shoulders with one another. Have the old and the young write devotional lessons together, play together, and pray together. Have them go on trips together. Have them visit other old folks together or young folks in hospitals. The Lord has made us "ready" right now. Celebrate and serve together in Christ.

Bonus! Just BE . . . BE-cause of Our Baptism!

The best way that young and old can minister together is to just BE! We are all people of God, loved, redeemed, and forgiven!

Colossians 3:12 says it so well, "As God's chosen, holy and dearly loved, clothe yourselves with compassion, kindness, humility, gentleness and patience" (NIV). Notice that the Lord first affirms us as His people, and then He tells us that, because we *are* God's people, we have been given these various gifts to share with others.

We are the people of God—whatever age we happen to be. We are simply asked to BE His people to others. Wow, what a God! What a gift! What a life!

DO BE DO BE DO! We are "do be do be do'ers" (with apologies to Frank Sinatra!) BE-cause we are God's people as a gift, we can now do His work among His people. What an *attitude* to have, in Christ.

Restating the Need—The Case for Older Adult/Grandparenting Ministries

- *Mass aging in the U.S.*

- *It is getting more and more obvious that there are more older adults around us than ever before. What a blessing this is!*

- *Are your worship services being attended by more and more older adults? More gray hairs and slower steppers? Great, that's a blessing!*

- *By 2030, there will be more people over age 65 than under age 18 in the United States. Of all of those over 65, 35 percent will be over 85. For every one hundred individuals ages 60–64 years old, there will be 80 people in their nineties! This is not a problem; this is an opportunity!*

- *Additionally, two-thirds of all people in human history who have ever reached age 65 or older, and three-fourths of all people in human history who have reached age 75 or older, are living today! Problem? No way! This is a promise, a gift, a blessing from the Lord!*

The Scriptures also strongly support the power and potential of older adults in ministry. Just listen, as one example, to Psalm 71:18, "So even to old age and gray hairs, O God, do not forsake me, until I proclaim Your might to another generation, Your power to all those to come."

The Lord is providing exciting opportunities for His Church to respond to the increasing number of older adults and grandparents in our congregations and communities. Blessings to you and your congregation as together we celebrate and enable these older saints of the Lord to proclaim and share the message of joy and peace and forgiveness with and to those younger folks around them, all in the name of the healing Christ.

Dr. Richard Bimler recently retired as president of Wheat Ridge Ministries. Rich is the author of numerous resources and a frequent speaker at events around the country.

Bibliography

Bayer, Les. *Devotions for the Chronologically Gifted.* St. Louis: Concordia Publishing House, 1999.

Bayer, Les. *Memories and Mentors.* Itasca, IL: Wheat Ridge Ministries, 2002.

Bimler, Rich. *Let There Be Laughter.* St. Louis: Concordia Publishing House, 1999.

Schoedel, Walt. *Engaging the Aging.* St. Louis: Lutheran Social Services.

Yount, David. *Celebrating the Rest of Your Life.* Minneapolis: Augsburg, 2005.

grandparenting

Passing on the Faith

BY AUDREY DUENSING-WERNER

O my people, hear my teaching; listen to the words of my mouth. I will open my mouth in parables, I will utter hidden things, things from old—what we have heard and known, what our fathers have told us. We will not hide them from their children; we will tell the next generation the praiseworthy deeds of the LORD, His power, and the wonders He had done. He decreed statutes for Jacob and established the law in Israel, which He commanded our forefathers to teach their children, so the next generation would know them, even the children yet to be born, and they in turn would tell their children. Then they would put their trust in God and would not forget His deeds but would keep His commands. (Psalm 78:1–7 NIV)

Life was short for the people of the psalmist's day, and they knew that they could take nothing with them when they died. But they knew they could leave something behind. They could pass on a gift with eternal significance.

The single greatest task and honor for parents in the psalmist's day was to pass on the faith, telling the next generation who God was, what He had done, and how He would have them to live, as well as His ultimate promise of a Savior. The people took seriously the importance of sharing God with the next generation. The greatest gift *we* to can give to our children is that they put their faith in the Lord. The greatest treasure we can place in their hearts is that they know what Christ did for them on the cross and at the empty tomb. He faced death head-on. He took our sins and the sins of the world upon Himself. He paid our debt and suffered our punishment. He conquered death when He rose from the dead.

Too many of our young people are at a loss for their identity. Too many of our children have no way to know they are loved by God. Too many of our youth are not told that God has a better idea concerning their hopelessness. These same youth are begging for more depth, for a God worth loving, and for a faith worth pursuing. Do you know what the resurrection means to our children? It means that they are forgiven, that they have hope. Death no longer has the final word in their life. It means they know a God who loves them even more than we do. It means they are His beloved.

Our children need to know that when they fail and fall into temptation and sin, they have a Savior who continually beckons them to come and receive His free gift of forgiveness won on the cross. That's a message that simply has to be shared.

One of my frustrations as a church leader is realizing that what happens or does not happen spiritually in the life of a child is directly related to what happens or does not happen spiritually in the home. We know that many parents are overwhelmed with raising children today. Parenting is complex and intense. There are multiple layers, learning styles, and family issues to muddle through—it can become overwhelming.

We know that our faith is a gift from God given to us in our Baptism. In Baptism we received the Holy Spirit, who continues to be at work in us to guide and comfort us. At the same time, parents, sponsors, *and* the church family promise to nurture the child's faith *with the help of God.* While research shows us that parents/family are most influential in the faith development of a child, parents are not left alone on this journey. God desires that we pass on our Christian faith to our children, and He will not leave us alone in the task. It is impossible, in fact, for parents to raise Christian children alone. Without the Holy Spirit we are powerless to pass on the faith at all. In addition, our sinful culture and the influences and powers that surround it are too much for us to handle alone. Parents need the support of the entire Christian community, along with the help of the Holy Spirit, to effectively pass on the faith.

Almost all of Scripture is addressed to communities. Jesus Himself called a group of disciples to continue passing on the Gospel. When He sent them out, He did not send them out alone. Yet many Christian parents either try to take on the task of passing on the faith all by themselves—which can be overwhelming—or they give away the power to share their faith with their children solely to schools, Sunday Schools, or church workers. God did not intend this to be an either/or, but a both/and. Passing on the faith must be done not only in the home, but also within the whole Christian community. We are partners in this process.

In Deuteronomy 6:1–9, God addresses the community:

These are the commands, decrees and laws the LORD your God directed me to teach you to observe in the land that you are crossing the Jordan to possess, so that you, your children and their children after them may fear the LORD your God as long as you live by keeping all His decrees and commands that I give you, and so that you may enjoy long life. Hear, O Israel, and be careful to obey so that it may go well with you and that you may increase greatly in a land flowing with milk and honey, just as the LORD, the God of your fathers, promised you. Hear, O Israel: The LORD our God, the LORD is one. Love the LORD your God with all your heart and with all your soul and with all your strength. These commandments that I give you today are to be upon your hearts. Impress them on your children. Talk about them when you sit at home and when you walk along the road, when you lie down and when you get up. Tie them as symbols on your hands and bind them on your foreheads. Write them on the doorframes of your houses and on your gates. (NIV)

In this Word from God, He calls the entire community to listen, to hear. Not individuals, but the entire community. In these verses, God tells parents they are not alone. The Lord is there with them, as well as the community.

These verses remind parents to talk about God's Word continually. To teach and teach, to repeat and repeat, over and over again, the phrases of the faith. We share the stories of the faith when they are at home and when they are not. Talking faith talk with your children when they lie down and when they rise again bookends every day with God's Word.

God intends that our children and grandchildren and great-grandchildren fear the Lord all the days of their life. This fear does not mean to be afraid of God, but to understand that it's only by God's grace that we avoid His wrath. "Fearing the Lord" helps us recognize the awesomeness of His loving nature and respond to that awesomeness in worship.

The Church's Role

As church leaders, and as part of the community of faith, we are partners in passing on the faith to children. How can we help parents to nurture the faith at home and as a community?

1. Modeling

The adage "actions speak louder than words" reminds us that what we demonstrate in our own actions speaks volumes to our children/youth. It is important that parents speak clearly that worship and Bible study is what your family does so that it's not questioned at all. Regularly sharing God's Word and Sacrament are elements that help you grow closer to Christ. If you say that regular participation in worship and Bible study are important, then it is important that your family worships regularly. Your words must match your actions, for children see and imitate those actions.

Make sure that whatever the age, children are welcome in worship and Bible study. Even if they don't understand all that is going on, they will soon learn rituals of the faith. Share with them important parts of worship, and model for them significant faith-connecting pieces such as prayer, offering, singing hymns, and so forth. If you say that an offering is giving God the firstfruits of what He gave you, then demonstrate that each Sunday by offering gifts back to God.

If you tell your child that Sunday School is important, model in the same way by attending a weekly Sunday School (adult Bible) class.

If you are not in the habit of worshiping and attending Bible study regularly, it's always good to start anew and make a family plan. Here are some practical ways that parents can help children/youth to be active participants in worship:

- *Make worship and Bible study a priority.*

- *Begin preparing for worship the night before—set out clothes, go to bed early, talk about the plan to attend worship.*

- *Arrive in time to sit together as a family. Sit where children can see.*

- *Make sure each family member receives a worship bulletin. Explain parts of the worship rituals before the service begins.*

- *Adults can be a great role model by entering worship with an attitude of reverence and joy.*

- *Expect the youth/child to participate in worship. Sing, pray, stand, recite, and so forth.*

- *Help children find hymns.*

- *Teach the children the liturgy at home, including the Lord's Prayer, the Apostles' Creed, Doxology, and others. Be ready to share what they mean to you personally.*

- *Quietly talk the children through what is going on throughout the worship service.*

- *Bring your Bibles and look up the Scriptures being read. Many bulletins have the Bible reading printed, but it is good to bring your own Bible and get in the habit of looking up verses and chapters so the child will know where to find them.*

- *After worship, talk about the service. Have the child listen for and then talk about one word in the sermon that they remember and what it means to them. Share the parts of the service in which God especially touched your heart and explain why.*

- *Encourage children to give an offering. Pass the plate to them.*

2. Tell the Faith Story

We are, as God's people, and as a community of faith, a part of God's living story today. He lives and works in us to share His message of hope and love and salvation to others. We are God's Church, God's story to His people. His living Word (Hebrews 4:12) is a drama, and we are a part of the unfinished story.

Begin telling children about Jesus early on. Tie those Bible stories of God's faithfulness to their hands and heart and bind them on their foreheads. Just as you would share popular children's stories with children, make Bible stories an important part of their reading repertoire early on—even in the womb (this is a good time to start practicing sharing every day). Open their children's Bible and read aloud stories of God's people, then open the "big people's" Bible and show them the same story in your Bible. When they are old enough to read, begin transitioning over to the "big people's" Bible, and reflect together on what things they heard, saw, smelled, and so forth as they read the story. Find stories of Christian heroes and heroines, martyrs of the faith and servants of the faith for them to read about.

Make faith talk a part of your everyday language. Just as you would verbally teach your child about what's right to touch and not to touch or what's right to say and not to say, make faith language just as much a part of your language, if not more so.

Share your faith story with your child. Sharing your faith with your family is great practice for sharing it with others and will become a natural part of your family conversation.

Share daily testimonies about how Gods worked in your life today. Then begin helping children see God's hand at work in every aspect of their life. Share with children every day how God is at work in their world *today*. Share personal testimonies passed down from generation to generation. Consider connecting children with people in your church or neighborhood who have faith stories to tell.

Without passing on the Gospel story, without sharing our faith stories, youth have nowhere to place themselves. They lack a nucleus of identity, a personality that has been formed by moral authority and mentoring models. Many young people have no sense of themselves and don't know who they are or whose they are. They constantly shift to fit into cultural stories of the times and satisfy the longing for an identity that was given to them when they were first created "in the image of God."

God's story is a living story. When the Word of God is opened up and read, it becomes alive. Families that immerse themselves in the biblical stories raise children who find their bearings and discover what it is to be a citizen of God's kingdom. Daily family devotions open up the minds of children to see sharing of food with the hungry, clothing the naked and sheltering the homeless, and being attentive to those in need. Sharing God's story produces children of character who reach out to others.

Some ways to begin sharing faith stories:

- *Share about a Sunday School teacher who showed Jesus' love in a special way and why.*

- *Share some of the faith stories that your parents or grandparents shared with you. Have you and your child record faith stories in a booklet.*

- *Share your favorite Bible story and tell why it is a favorite.*

- *Every time you go to a store or when you are out and about, play a game with your child/youth to find something you see that shows God's presence.*

- *Connect your young person(s) with elderly people in the congregation who can share their faith stories.*

3. Relationships

Prof. Gerry Coleman from Concordia University in Bronxville, New York, says the most important thing for God's people to remember as they interact with each other and those around them is to focus on three things: Relationships! Relationships! Relationships!

Relationship with God. Once again, this brings us back to modeling and community. Spending time in personal prayer and devotion can be integral in showing little ones that God is more than facts—He is the Christ. To you, Christ Jesus is the One who holds your heart close to His. You are His child. Showing a child that seeking to know and understand the God who loves them is what you desire most is modeling conversation with God; it's modeling time with God; it's modeling a relationship with God; and it's showing them how the living Word works in your heart to share Christ with others.

Relationships within the family. More than any other thing, we must help families develop their relationship skills. When relationships are good in the family, then values, morals, faith, and so forth are looked upon as being good. A good healthy relationship with a son/daughter helps the young person feel safe about asking the hard faith questions. Talking through life struggles and how God supports us on our journey helps others turn to Him in all times and helps them know a stronger faith in Him.

Family relationships are complex, but helping families work through conflict, communication, and caring for each other will go a long way in connecting their children to faith in Christ Jesus. As families work through the ups and downs of relationship building, they nurture a child's faith walk in a powerful way.

Relationships within the community of faith. The most convincing testimony to the existence and grace of God for our children will be God's love by the Christian community and testimonies of faith and actions of individuals of the faith community to young people and children.

4. Financially

One hundred percent of what we have is God's. Help young people recognize that our material possessions, our talents, and all the years of our life belong to God. God intends for all those things to be used to give Him honor and praise. Sharing with children/youth that giving to God's work as part of God's community is a privilege and not a burden is integral. Help your children/youth see that you trust God to take care of all your needs and that giving back what is already His is a great time to celebrate.

Make a financial commitment to your children's spiritual future. Set money aside for spiritual events. I know there are many costs with raising children/youth, but what can be more important than a close relationship with Jesus? Show children/youth that Christian education and spiritual-growth events are worth budgeting and saving for.

- *Help a young person/child learn early how to tithe: 10% God, 10% savings, 80% other.*

- *Provide opportunities for your young person to share in the cost of Christian camp, mission trips, and other experiences.*

- *Ask your child to begin saving money to help give a scholarship to someone who may need financial help for camp or a mission trip.*

- *Adopt a missionary family and provide an item for each month—maybe diapers for a baby or water for the family.*

5. Experience

We know that children and youth learn about their faith through experience. Being part of a worshiping community provides the opportunity for them to learn the language, rituals, and stories of their faith. They find a place to belong, where people outside their immediate family love and affirm them. It is important to integrate children and youth into the worshiping community and provide them with opportunities to think deeply about the meaning of the things that happen to them and the meaning of the stories of their faith.

- *Explore the spiritual gifts of youth/children, and place them in a congregational ministry where they can serve using those gifts.*

- *Provide service opportunities to get in the habit of helping the needy, the poor, and the homeless.*

- *Make the children/youth aware of disaster areas or poverty-stricken communities, and make a family plan to help where needed.*

- *Make giving to the needy in the community a priority. Examples: angel tree, school supplies, prison fellowship, food pantries.*

6. Music

The music and hymnody of the Church have played an important part in teaching the faith for generations. It not only teaches great doctrine, but also reinforces biblical faith stories. There are CDs and tapes available that play traditional hymnody as well as some beautiful new contemporary pieces that pass on the faith in a powerful way. Research shows that music plays an integral part in memorizing and recall. Using music as a tool to share faith is a wonderful way to pass on the faith and share favorite pieces with the child/youth that give comfort in times of trials. Pointing out pieces of the liturgy that are in Scripture and/or using songs to memorize Scripture is another good way to reinforce the faith story.

7. Grace

Make grace talk and grace actions part of the home and faith community. Keep the focus on the love and forgiveness and the presence and promises of Christ.

When my niece Sydney was just four years old, my sister Rochelle reprimanded and punished Sydney for something inappropriate she had done. Sydney immediately said, "I'm sorry, Momma." Rochelle then, just a few steps away, sat down on a nearby bench, pulled her close, and said, "Sydney, you know that even when you mess up, Momma loves you and Momma forgives you?" Sydney responded, "Yes, Momma." Then Rochelle added, out loud, in the middle of a major department store, "You know that when you mess up, Jesus loves you even more than Momma does." Sydney's eyes got brighter. She smiled and then began singing, without any hesitation, "Jesus loves me this I know for the Bible tells me so . . ." There they sat on a bench in a store in Des Moines, Iowa, and sang "Jesus Loves Me" together. But here's what's even neater than that grace-filled moment—a woman walked past as they were singing, and Sydney pointed at her and said, "And He loves you too." That's grace talk!

- *Model grace by speaking it out loud not only to your children and family, but to the community of faith as well, so that your children see you follow through with others also.*

- *Confess openly and practice a ritual of "You're forgiven by me in the name of Jesus Christ."*

DCE Audrey Duensing-Werner serves as director of youth ministries at Cross View Lutheran Church in Edina, Minnesota.

celebrations

10

Family Ministry Celebrations

BY KAY MEYER

And these words that I command you today shall be on your heart. You shall teach them diligently to your children, and shall talk of them when you sit in your house, and when you walk by the way, and when you lie down, and when you rise. (Deuteronomy 6:6–7)

The family was created by God (Genesis 1:27–28; 2:18, 21–25) to be the fundamental and foundational place for spiritual nurture. Yet statistics document that the family in the United States is in serious trouble. The Gallup Poll revealed that households headed by unmarried partners grew by almost 72 percent during the past decade. Households headed by single mothers or fathers increased by 25 percent and 62 percent, respectively, and for the first time, the nuclear family dropped below 25 percent of households. Thirty-three percent of all babies were born to unmarried women, compared to only 3.8 percent in 1940. Other studies show that cohabitation increased by almost 1,000 percent from 1960 to 1998, and that households headed by same-sex couples are soaring.

Congregations must find more and better ways to partner with the home and offer hope and help to families. Those that do this find multiple blessings! Families today struggle with many challenges. Churches must be responsive to a myriad of family needs and help individuals learn to share their faith within the home. Besides strengthening Christian families, congregational family ministry is a tool for reaching beyond the walls of the church to those who do not know Christ!

Congregational leaders must make decisions about the type of family ministry they will address. Small congregations cannot do everything. But, family ministry is broad and deep. The mission: to equip individuals and their families to grow in faith and pass that faith on to the next generation. Encouraging parents, grandparents, godparents, aunts, and uncles to be in the Word lies at the core of effective family ministry.

Family life begins in the womb and ends in the tomb. Stages of family life include the newly married couple, the couple expecting their first child, the young couple with several children, the single parent, couples and singles with teenagers, couples and singles with children in college, couples and singles that have never had children, couples and singles with grown children, couples, singles, widows, and widowers with grandchildren living near and far, and blended families.

How can congregations partner with the home? Offer parenting programs, support groups, divorce recovery groups, and Bible studies. Plan celebrations and milestones that involve the entire congregation!

Congregational leaders should be aware that twenty-five years of research has identified six traits that build strong, healthy families. Think about how your congregation might help families grow in each of these areas.

1. *Commitment to each other's welfare and happiness*

2. *Appreciation and affection for each other (Genesis 2:23–24; Psalm 127:3–4)*

3. *Positive communication (Ephesians 6:1–4)*

4. *Spending time together (Deuteronomy 6:7; Proverbs 22:6)*

5. *Spiritual well-being (Acts 2:38–39; Deuteronomy 6:7; Ephesians 6:4)*

6. *The ability to cope with stress and crisis (Ephesians 6:4; 1 Thessalonians 2:11)*

Model Family Devotions for Parents

We will not hide them from their children; we will tell the next generation the praiseworthy deeds of the LORD, His power, and the wonders He has done. (Psalm 78:4 NIV)

Often families don't have devotions in the home because they don't know how. Congregational leaders need to model how to present devotions in the home. Conversations occur as we talk, travel, sit in the home, and lie down at night.

family ministry celebrations

Encourage parents to begin the process of nurturing their children's faith within the home.

1. *Celebrate Baptism! God reaches down through the water and the Word and makes the child His, bestowing faith. "Repent and be baptized every one of you in the name of Jesus Christ for the forgiveness of your sins, and you will receive the gift of the Holy Spirit. For the promise is for you and for your children" (Acts 2:38–39).*

2. *Teach children to pray! My grandson Seth loves to lead the mealtime prayers. His other grandmother taught him this age-appropriate prayer, "ABC, 123. Thank You, God, for feeding me! Amen." Congregation leaders can help families learn prayers to use at mealtimes and bedtime.*

3. *Encourage parents to take children to Sunday School and church. Remind parents that worship begins the night before the service. Make sure things are ready in advance. Lay out the church clothes the children will wear.*

4. *Be honest. Help parents recognize that the home is the most difficult place to live our faith. Encourage families to confess their sins to each other and pray for each other so that they may be healed (James 5:16). "Get rid of all bitterness, rage and anger, brawling and slander, along with every form of malice. Be kind and compassionate to one another, forgiving each other, just as in Christ God forgave you" (Ephesians 4:31–32 NIV).*

5. *Encourage parents and grandparents to talk about faith with their children and youth. Begin when they are young.*

Conversations about faith issues can arise easily. The following are other examples of how talking with children about their faith can occur:

My husband and I visited our family in River Forest, Illinois. We attended church together. My grandson Seth was almost three years old. Seth's parents took him to Communion with them. The pastor, who baptized Seth, always blesses the children. He places his hand upon their head and reminds them of their Baptism and what Christ has done for them. After returning to the pew, Seth turned to his mother and said, "Mama, Pastor said Jesus washed me clean." He took his hands and pretended to wash his face. After the service my daughter told me what he'd said. I leaned down to talk with Seth and said, "Seth, your mommy told me you said Jesus washed us all clean." He responded, "No, Jesus washed *me* clean!" Seth understood the message of forgiveness was for *him*! Forgiveness because of Christ through the waters of Baptism was comprehended.

Four-year-old Annie heard her parents talking about angels after a Bible study. Later she asked her grandfather, "Grandpa, angels helped Jesus when He needed strength in that garden didn't they? Does God still sends angels today to help us?" Grandpa answered, "Wow, what a good question, Annie. Let's take a walk and think about this some more. How does God use angels?"

Sometimes we won't have all the answers. That's okay. Help parents understand that their children will ask questions for which they don't have answers. Encourage parents to be honest. Have them tell their children they don't know. Then go and find out!

One Good Friday our extended family again attended worship together. I sat next to my son-in-law David. As the Tenebrae service progressed, he quietly explained what was occurring and why to four-year-old Seth. Seth took it all in. On Easter morning, Seth asked, "Papa, is Jesus God?" "Yes!" David said. "What a great question!"

Today's families face obstacles as they establish family devotions. The major obstacle seems to be time. No one has enough time. We must take time! A wide range in the ages of children is another obstacle. It's difficult to have an age-appropriate devotion when you have a three-year-old, an eight-year-old, and an eleven-year-old. Encourage parents to alternate the type of devotion they use. Ask older children to help plan the devotion for the three-year-old. The tendency to declare Law and little or no Gospel is another obstacle. Parents (and sometimes even church leaders) present the Law effectively, but they forget the Gospel. The Gospel must be at the forefront of devotions within the home! Finally, our sinful nature makes it easy to say, "I just can't lead devotions" or "I'm too tired." How do we overcome these obstacles? By confessing our sins, asking for God's help, and beginning anew!

Keep devotions short and age-appropriate with young children. Use interactive learning. Ask questions. Play games. Use concrete items. Do or make something together, and then talk about God. Take a walk and talk about God's marvelous creation. Ask children to see how many things they can find that begin with *A* through *Z* that God made. Pray together. Help older children begin private devotions. Make sure they have a Bible that is age-appropriate, and read the stories with them regularly.

Celebrating Traditions and Rituals throughout the Church Year

I host an hour-long radio program each weekend for Family Shield Ministries. On a recent program, I interviewed Jill Hasstedt, director of family ministry at Zion Lutheran Church in Belleville, Illinois, and Krista Young, director of youth and family ministry at Ascension Lutheran Church in St. Louis. We discussed their congregations and how they partner with the home. Some of the information that follows is taken from that interview.

Why should congregations focus on family ministry? Congregations that partner with the home assist parents in keeping the promise they made at their child's Baptism. Milestones and celebrations keep the parents and the child connected to the Lord and others within the church.

What are milestones? Milestones are congregationally sponsored programs. They equip and nurture the entire family. Milestones are times to encourage and strengthen children's faith and involve their parents, godparents, grandparents, and other adult members of the congregation in the faith journey. Some congregations that have been having milestones for many years hold from six to eight milestones each year within the parish. Those involved tell leaders to begin with one or two and gradually add more each year.

Most milestones begin with an educational program for parents. Often the children and youth are also involved. The final phase brings the parents and child to a church service together. At the appropriate time, all of them are invited forward during the service. The child/youth is given a gift and encouraged in the faith journey.

The milestone process begins with a letter that is mailed to families that have children in the age bracket that the event will address. A follow-up telephone call is made to the families to explain the process further and encourage them to partici-pate. Some type of program or event is held to educate the parents and other significant adults. Children and youth are also often involved. The final part of the milestone event is held at a worship service. The parents and their child come for-ward during the service. The children usually receive a gift as part of the presenta-tion. That gift is personalized with a note from their parents and/or other adults.

Some congregations purchase the Bibles and/or gifts for the parents. Others allow the parents, godparents, or grandparents to purchase the gift. Gifts are age-appropriate and may include Bibles or religious books. When children begin Sunday School at age 3, they receive a children's Bible. At age 7, they receive another Bible that they can read themselves. Each time the children and their parents are reminded of their Baptism and the faith God gave them. Before the gifts are given, each adult is encouraged to write a personal message inside the Bible or book and highlight a favorite Bible verse. The children treasure these gifts and read the messages again and again.

Some congregations have volunteers make a small wooden chest called a "FaithChest." It can be given to the child at his/her Baptism or even at confirmation. The child keeps religious paperwork, the Baptism candle, and other important religious objects as reminders of important milestones. The Youth and Family Institute has instructions for creating a "FaithChest" on their Web site: www.youthandfamilyinstitute.org.

Each congregation and its leaders decide what type of educational event to hold. Some have Bible studies for two weeks, some for three weeks, and some are one day. Milestones allow the adults in the child's life to be reminded of their promise during Baptism to raise the children to know and love Jesus. As the parents and significant adults attend and listen to the Word, the Holy Spirit works in their life. Their own faith grows!

Milestones allow congregations to be family-friendly. During our interview, Jill said, "It is incredible pastoral care. Each family receives a letter and a follow-up telephone call. They attend the sessions in preparation for the milestone event, meet other Christians, and grow in their own relationship with the Lord. They are far less likely to fall away."

Hasstedt and Young coordinate the milestone events at their congregations and rely on volunteers to help. A committed and trained volunteer could also be in charge of these educational/nurturing events at congregations that have no director of Christian education. Hasstedt uses volunteers who have gone through the event with their children in previous years. Her congregation currently marks five milestones; Young's has three milestones. Both plan to expand the milestone events until they have six to eight each year.

Getting the Word of God into Children's Hands and Hearts

"And how from childhood you have been acquainted with the sacred writings, which are able to make you wise for salvation through faith in Christ Jesus" (2 Timothy 3:15).

Consider the following examples of celebrations and milestones that you might host in your congregation:

So You're Having a Baby

"O LORD, I beg You, let the man of God You sent to us come again to teach us how to bring up the boy who is to be born" (Judges 13:8).

As you consider milestones, look at existing programs within your parish. One program that has been used for years in the Lutheran Church is the Cradle Roll. Cradle Roll resources are available from Concordia Publishing House. Parents receive regular mailings during the first three years of their child's life. It helps new parents stay connected to the church and shares appropriate resources that will help them raise their child to know and love Jesus.

Baptism Classes for Parents and Godparents

Offer classes to educate parents and godparents about Baptism. Teach them what God does in Baptism, how to select a godparent, and what will happen during the worship service. Share devotional material they can use in the home. Parents and godparents should be people of faith in the child's life. Since fellowship is important, begin or end the classes with coffee and dessert.

Baptism for Infants and Adults Brings Faith

In Baptism, God reaches down through the water and the Word and bestows faith. Concordia Lutheran Church in Kirkwood, Missouri, encourages parents and godparents to help children understand the importance of Baptism. Like many churches, they give the parents a white candle and share ways parents and godparents can use this candle throughout the years. The pastor might take just a few minutes following the Baptism to say, "Here is a candle you can use to help your child remember his/her Baptism. Light it on good days and on bad days. Also light it on their Baptism birthday. Celebrate this day throughout their life!"

Baptism Birthdays

When were you baptized? How can congregations encourage parents, godparents, and grandparents to celebrate Baptism birthdays? Baptism is a significant event in the life of each believer. It marks the day that we became God's own child through water and the Word.

For Christ also suffered once for sins, the righteous for the unrighteous, that He might bring us to God, being put to death in the flesh but made alive in the spirit. . . . Baptism, which corresponds to this, now saves you, not as a removal of dirt from the body but as an appeal to God for a good conscience, through the resurrection of Jesus Christ. (1 Peter 3:18, 21)

Our daughter and son-in-law are godparents to Savanna, who lives five hours from them. But her Baptism birthday is important. They either travel to see her or send a special gift. One year they recorded a video and mailed it to her. In the video they told Savanna about her Baptism and why it is so important. They got this idea from a list of ideas that Savanna's church gave them on the day she was baptized.

A Beginning Sunday School Milestone

Children begin Sunday School when they are two or three years old. Beginning Sunday School provides an opportunity to have a milestone event. Many congregations already invite parents to attend the first Sunday School class. Consider expanding this to become a milestone. Involve parents and children. Bring entire families forward during a worship service before the first Sunday School class each fall. Give children an age-appropriate Bible or Arch Book. Invite the parents to highlight their favorite Bible verse or story and write a personal message inside the Bible or book.

The Prayer Milestone for Five- or Six-Year-Olds

Ascension Lutheran Church recently began a new milestone called the Prayer Milestone, which targets five- and six-year-old children and their parents. Families are invited to a two-week Bible study before the milestone event. During the first Bible study, the DCE reviewed what the Small Catechism says about teaching children to pray. She answered questions that parents had about prayer. It also included a Bible study on Simeon and Anna.

The second week they brainstormed prayers that they could use in the home and ideas that would be used in home devotional times. Following the sessions, each family was encouraged to find an "Anna" or "Simeon" within the congregation who would pray for their child and family.

The next week, the child, parents, and the new prayer partner came forward during the worship service. Each child was given a prayer book. Parents and prayer partners wrote a blessing inside it. They then gave the gift to the child. Many took time to hug the children and again remind them of their Baptism.

This milestone became an intergenerational event. One prayer partner said, "I am so honored and touched to be asked to be a part of this family and remember them in prayer!" New relationships were formed that will last a lifetime.

A Milestone for Second Graders

The process for each milestone is similar to the details above, but the age of the child changes. Some congregations offer a milestone for second graders. Students and parents gather once a week for three weeks to review the books of the Bible and highlight key verses. The congregational leaders make the gathering fun! When they get to the story of Noah, they might sing a song about him. If they run out of time, they give the Bible verses to the parents and ask them to highlight them at home. All books of the Bible are highlighted. It is a community-building event. Parents meet each other and form strong friendships. Parents share stories and observe other children. This helps them realize that they are not alone in the parenting process.

When the milestone day arrives, parents give the open Bible to their child and write a blessing inside it. Then they give their child a hug.

Jill shared a powerful story of the impact of these events. She explained that one of her second graders went through this milestone while her father was dying. Before the day of the milestone, her father died. This young child requested that one of the Bible verses from Jonah that she and her father had highlighted during the family gathering be part of her father's funeral. The pastor used the verse for the funeral sermon.

Confirmation Celebrations and Retreat

Some congregations have confirmation retreats. Talking about our faith with children and youth is important. Some years ago, I went on a confirmation retreat with my son's class at a local retreat center. During the two-day retreat, we broke into small groups to talk about faith issues. During one discussion, a student shared, "I don't know if my parents believe in God or not. I've never heard them talk about God." How sad! Our children should overhear conversations about faith issues. This helps them understand that our faith is real. It will also spur them to ask questions about God and His Word.

A Confirmation Milestone

Zion Lutheran Church uses secret prayer partners for seventh and eighth graders. During the year prior to their confirmation, they receive anonymous cards and small gifts. They finally meet their secret prayer partners at a confirmation gathering. This process provides another way for adults to support the youth of their congregation. The confirmation students, parents, and prayer partners gather to make a confirmation banner.

High School Graduation Blanket/Quilt Milestone

Zion has a unique milestone that congregations might want to duplicate. I t is designed for students who are going to graduate from high school. A letter explaining the milestone event is sent to the student and parents. A church volunteer makes a follow-up telephone call inviting student and parents to participate in this evening milestone event in April. Dessert is served. A panel of parents who have gone through this phase of family life answer questions. They talk about challenges regarding the spiritual life of an adult child. Each family makes a stadium blanket for their child. The blankets are personalized in various ways. Some use handprints of parents, grandparents, other significant adults, and siblings in the child's life. Each parent writes a blessing that is given with the blanket.

A date for giving the blankets to the graduates in front of the rest of the congregation is set. Parents and teens bring the blankets they made to the worship service. Participants come forward to the front of the church. There the pastor says, "When you were a baby, your parents brought you to Baptism, and God made you His child. They wrapped you in a blanket. Today they give you a new blanket. This blanket reminds you that God still wraps you in His love. As you move to this next stage of life, remember that your parents still love you."

As teenagers graduate and go to college or into the service, they take their blanket with them. The blanket serves as a constant reminder that God walks with them and that their families love them too.

Other Parish Activities Involving the Entire Family

Your congregation probably has traditions that could be developed into family activities for the parish. Review your traditions, and see what might be expanded to accomplish a milestone.

Consider intergenerational events! Did you know that the church is one of the few places where intergenerational events still occur outside of the family? Intergenerational activities are important. Plan one for your congregation. Why not consider planning an intergenerational Vacation Bible School or a summer festival? Many congregations have done this and will share plans with other congregations. Because many older persons do not live near their grandchildren, these events can help children and youth become acquainted with people of all ages.

Family Sunday School Events

Ascension Lutheran Church in St. Louis holds four family Sunday School events every year. A Palm Sunday gathering is one of them. Parents are invited to attend Sunday School with their children. They also invite other members of the congregation to attend and help families with more than one child. In this way, it becomes an intergenerational event.

The Word of God is read, songs are sung, and participants pray together. The youth present a puppet show. Then the children and parents make a flowerpot with four candles. One candle is purple, and three are white. Grass is put inside. A bow is put on the flowerpot. Snacks are served.

As they leave, the families are given a devotional booklet to use at home with the flowerpot for family devotions.

Annual Family Retreat or Camping Trip

When my three children were young, about twenty families from our congregation went on a two-day camping trip. It was advertised in the church bulletin and was open to everyone. We had a great time, visited some local attractions together, played volleyball, sang songs, and cooked hot dogs and s'mores over the campfire. Several of us even had an opportunity to witness to a couple from Germany camping next to us. Be sure to include time for Bible study and devotions together, but also allow time for individual families to spend time together.

General Suggestions for Church and Family Leaders

Encourage parents to set up a devotional center at home. Use play dough to make a holder for a candle or a cross for the altar. Allow the children to decide how to decorate the altar. In devotions, include a time of confession and forgiveness. Model how to do this in Bible studies and special classes at church. Give parents simple suggestions they can begin to incorporate into their devotions at home. Read a Bible storybook. Show them ways you can use this at home.

Use children's sermons to present ideas or words for children to focus on during the sermon or the rest of the service. Print out the Scripture lessons in the bulletin each week. Include in the bulletin the lessons and at least one hymn that will be sung the following week so parents can teach their children the hymn, the liturgy, and the lesson for the coming week. Encourage parents to help their children memorize the liturgy and Bible verses.

In your congregational newsletter, include ideas for families on how to share their faith within the home. Consider designing bulletin inserts or purchasing ones that share ideas for the home. Create an e-mail newsletter just for families, and put ideas on your church's Web site. Use suggestions for family activities found in your Sunday School curriculum. Remember that godparents and grandparents don't always get to see these ideas. Grandparents are sometimes the only ones sharing their faith with the children and youth.

Family Service and Servant Projects

"I am reminded of your sincere faith, a faith that dwelt first in your grandmother Lois and your mother Eunice and now, I am sure, dwells in you as well" (2 Timothy 1:5).

Family service projects are a way to thank God! Here are some things you might do with your family:

- *Go Christmas caroling to members who are confined.*

- *Rake leaves and help with chores; shovel snow for neighbors or relatives.*

- *Go to the store for elderly neighbors when the weather is bad.*

- *Make cookies and take them to someone who is ill. When you visit, give them a homemade card and tell them you are praying for them.*

Congregational leaders can make a difference in the lives of the families they serve. Begin with one of the suggestions in this chapter. Pray for God's wisdom. Ask volunteers for assistance. And expand your ministry by offering family celebrations and milestones!

Kay Meyer is founder and president of Family Shield Ministries, Inc. She also hosts Family Shield, a weekly radio program heard in the St. Louis area (www.familyshieldministries.com).

Building a Support Network

BY JILL HASSTEDT

Support systems are complex structures of personal, organizational, spiritual, and emotional support. They "carry the weight" of a ministry in ways that prevent it or the people and families being served by it from failing or falling during stressful times. Support systems don't just happen. Like any structure, they can be designed and built, improved, strengthened, remodeled, and added on to.

A support system for family ministry is like the classic analogy of the three-legged stool. Without the support of all three legs, the stool lacks stability. Here are three areas where it is important to build support:

1. *Support for God's people in and from all kinds of families—dealing with crisis, life changes, and special issues*

2. *Support for the ministry—policies and procedures*

3. *Support for the workers—volunteer and professional (including numbers 1 and 2 above)*

Leg 1: Support for God's People in and from All Kinds of Families

Family systems are under stress. That's not a new thing in history. It goes all the way back to Adam and Eve. (What's more stressful than being barred from Paradise or having one child murder another?) There's not a home in your town that doesn't need your support in some way.

How do you craft support when you're dealing with big things such as life change, sudden crisis, or special issues unique to your people? A little advance work can help, but things will come up that you never even thought of preparing for. Where do you start? Keep reading.

A rule of thumb: Never do something alone that you could involve others in doing with you (even if it's faster and easier the other way around). Your goal is to expand the circle of influence, to equip future leaders and advocates, and to begin to create a mind-set for family ministry that will infiltrate every area of church life.

Just Start Somewhere!

1. *Determine the hot issues in your setting. Focus on the families God has already given you. If you serve them well, you'll also serve their friends and the guests they bring to church with them. Remember, you're entering people's lives at moments when they are most vulnerable and open to change—moments when the Holy Spirit might be working in their hearts to hear Him for the first time. This is truly the work of the church! What are the areas where families in your church are in crisis, are experiencing life change across the life span, or where there are special issues? See the **Leg 1 Support Chart** at the end of this chapter to help define possible issues.*

2. *What is your church already doing? Some samples are listed on the **Leg 1 Support Chart**. Programs used by other churches are listed in italics to get you started. You may not be doing those things listed, but you are doing others. Make the list your own. Recruiting a team to work with you on this process will begin widening the circle of support for family ministry.*

3. *Celebrate! The typical church's "cradle to grave ministry" is already supporting families in many ways. Tell others what you discovered. Thank your pastor for all he does! Commend the work that others have done before you. However, it's almost never enough, or you wouldn't be reading this chapter. So . . .*

4. *Begin to strengthen, repair, and remodel the support system(s) already in place! Don't forget to look at areas where support is not working or is dangerously tottering—demolition may be in order. Maybe a new addition is needed. Think years, not weeks or months. Over time, you'll see a huge difference. Every building project begins with one shovel of dirt turned over. Identify one area where you can make an impact soon, even if its just a few well-placed bulletin announcements. See the list of suggested bulletin announcements and ideas below for specific examples. Identify areas where you would like to begin to make a longer-term impact.*

Bulletin Announcements and Ideas That Build Support for Children in Worship

Don't assume that even the most obvious and basic things concerning worship are understood or taught at home. The suggested bulletin announcements below explain why raisins are a bad snack choice for worship (they get squished into the carpet) and suggest better ones; encourage parents to practice the Lord's Prayer at home and then make a point of saying it together in worship; give tips for packing church busy bags for tiny tots, and so forth. The list could go on forever, but the point is that parents appreciate the tips and the education process is good for the whole family.

Tips for Children in Worship—Never Underestimate the Value of a Cheerio!

We love having little ones in worship! Little ones wiggle, and any parent who's ever wrangled a new walker through church knows the value of a strategically placed snack. Cheerios and fish crackers are a great choice because they're portable, nonperishable, and easy to pack (and those who clean the church appreciate the easy vacuum cleanup). Help us keep the church clean by avoiding snacks that can get squished in carpeting (raisins) or leave a sticky mess behind.

Tips for Children in Worship—Praying

Even the youngest among us can begin to learn worship behavior. Parents and grandparents can help. Show little ones how to fold their hands and bow their heads when it's time to pray. Parents with infants can put their hands around their infant's hands to help. Start saying the Lord's Prayer together every night at bedtime. In just a few weeks, even toddlers can begin saying it with us in church.

Tips for Children in Worship—Wiggle Tamer Bags

We love having children in worship, but if the littlest ones need some wiggle tamers to get through worship, may we suggest the following: Bible story board books or touch-and-feel books, a Bible story coloring book, small stuffed animals with religious significance (lambs, donkeys, roosters, and so forth). Don't know where to find these? We're hosting a Concordia Christian Book Fair next week (dates and time here). We're including ten-minute workshops (on the hour and half hour) for parents on how to make, pack, and use a Wiggle Tamer Bag. Join us.

Tips for Children in Worship—Restroom and Drink Breaks

New walkers may need a turn around the narthex during the sermon, and a toddler may need a restroom visit. By the time a child is in kindergarten or first grade, it's a great idea to remind them that restroom breaks should be the exception, not the rule. Going to the restroom before church is a good idea. When a break is necessary, children and adults are encouraged to exit on the side aisles to minimize distraction to other worshipers.

Tips for Children in Worship—May I Sit with My Friends?

We think worship should be a family activity. Encourage connection with friends at other times, or agree with other parents that you will allow your child to sit with their family or their child to sit with yours. We'd like to gently discourage children and students of any age from sitting together in groups without an adult. Even with the best intentions, the potential for distraction is just too great. It's not a bad idea to avoid temptation.

Ideas for Involving Families in Worship

- *Teach worship in worship—most of your adult worshipers don't even know what kyrie means, why the pastor wears unique clothes, or what a parament is. Try a "liturgical minute" every week and teach the mechanics, vocabulary, and reason behind the rituals. Over time, the impact will be incredible.*

- *Emergency Wiggle Tamers—harried parents of toddlers often forget Cheerios, soft books, and crayons. Provide a basket of appropriate items for families to borrow. Invite donations inspired by experience.*

- *Consider including prayers for children or their prayer requests in the service.*

- *Appeal to all the senses—educators know that people have different learning styles. Varying how you teach (or preach or worship) will help make sure the message gets through. How can worshipers, children and adults alike, use their talents to create an environment that is a delight to the Lord and enhances worship? (What can be seen, heard, touched, and tasted?)*

- *Include one point in the sermon specifically for children. Be very obvious. "Now I want the little ones to listen to this . . ."*

Plan how you will refer those with needs or problems beyond your expertise or financial capabilities to qualified professionals or other agencies of assistance. Do not assume that those you serve will have the skills to identify and access sources of assistance or the presence of mind to use those skills in stressful times. Your role will be to walk alongside them in the process of connecting to these services. Note the following:

- *The health insurance of the person you're assisting may require selection of a counselor from a list of preferred providers. You can walk along-side people who need help connecting, but they will have to make the call and will probably need to speak with a specialized screener who certifies initial visits. Note that your role will be limited by privacy laws.*

- *Many people do not have mental-heath coverage, but there are often sliding-scale fees based on financial need.*

- *Screen counselors and other care providers in your area in advance. A phone call asking for consultation regarding referrals in the future is usually all that's needed. Keep a detailed file page for each provider, and update this annually. (See the Screening Form found at the end of this chapter.)*

- *If there seems to be an agreement in beliefs, what is the potential for forming a partnership? If you refer people to them, will they discount their fee?*

building a support network

Basics

- *If they are unwilling to speak with you, do not refer others to them. Keep a form on file for each provider you have screened.*

- *Consider a Christian counselor. Check with the American Association of Christian Counselors (www.aacc.net). The code of ethics for the AACC is typically more stringent than the American Counseling Association's (ACA). A section on their Web site identifies counselors by zip code. Not all AACC members are trained counselors.*

- *An excellent resource for those who have not had a lot of experience with outside services is When and How to Use Mental Health Resources (Kenneth C. Haugk, Stephen Ministries, 2000), available from www.stephenministries.com. For a comprehensive program of lay care in your congregation, consider implementing the Stephen Ministry program.*

- *You will likely refer people to agencies of support for reasons other than mental-health care and counseling. These include state or county human services (housing, Medicaid, employment), support groups, food banks, debt-reduction assistance programs, hospice, home health care, and so on. Many communities have already compiled detailed lists of providers in book form. Ask around among providers in the area to see if this is the case. Use the Agency Referral Form at the end of the chapter to add specific information for these support agencies.*

Leg 2: Support for the Ministry

Well-Crafted Systems, Policies, and Procedures

While much of this topic is covered in other chapters, a few points bear repeating here. Family ministry is at its best when it is part of the overall flavor or mind-set of a congregation. It should weave its way through every area of congregation life so that in Sunday School, youth ministry, adult education, pastoral care, elders, school board, personnel, and even properties or trustees, there is forethought for family nurturing.

That kind of infiltrative support can take a decade to build, so initially someone or some group needs to act as advocate, instructor, research disseminator, organizer, and planner for family ministry. Adopting, sharing, and using a set of guiding principles for family ministry can further the process as ministries in your congregation study and absorb them. You can write these yourself or adapt them from other sources. The process of doing so will help create direction and momentum, not to mention some great discussion. See Principles for Family Ministry at the end of this chapter.

Anticipating potential problems, pitfalls, and needs shows great care for those you serve. Putting policies and procedures in writing creates a vital support structure for family ministry. While these can always be changed, they also create a map to follow and a foundation. They ensure safety and communicate boundaries. These should be printed, taught, shared, and revised as needed.

Policies allow planning teams to function without consistently asking for permission to continue. They also give some assurance of quality and accountability. Procedures identify and outline the "how to" part of an event. Procedures might include forms that need to be filled out or steps to follow in the completion of a task. Both deal with vital concerns and should ideally be put in place before you need them.

- *Will sick children be allowed in the nursery?*

- *What procedures will be used to notify a parent that a child is sick?*

- *How will fund-raising be handled? To whom will accounts be submitted for review?*

- *How will confidentiality be guarded?*

- *How long does someone have to be a member before being allowed to volunteer with children?*

- *Do all families attending the servant event have to show proof of primary health-care insurance? What if an uninsured family wants to participate?*

- *Do drivers for events have to show proof of insurance?*

- *Will medical information forms be required for the adult trips?*

- *Should child safety guidelines be displayed in the narthex?*

Pick any area of family ministry, and there's bound to be problems that could be prevented or minimized with a little forethought. Again, think in terms of months or years here, but do get started. Don't let a lack of written policies hamstring your ministry to families. Keep going. Chances are different ministries at your church may already have their own smaller policy manuals, but no one has collected and compiled these with some concern for uniformity and eye to family friendliness.

Policies and procedures should be reviewed, adapted, and approved by a team or committee formed for this purpose. Your church's insurance company might have specific requirements. Following a standard format and compiling these in a place where they won't be lost is also important.

Leg 3: Support for the Workers

The church seeking to build a comprehensive ministry to families models family-friendly policies for its own workers and is a leader in doing so in our society. It's a "walk the talk" issue and can't be ignored.

Biblically the mandate is quite clear—professional church workers and their families are to be models of family life (see 1 Timothy 3:1–12). That doesn't mean they have to be perfect. We all live under God's grace. But it does call for them to model healthy living, balanced lives, and to respond in positive ways when problems occur (as they do in *all* families). That doesn't happen without some intentional and loving support from the faith family they serve, including the following:

- *Adequate living wage*

- *Paid sick leave (which may also be used for dependent care)*

- *Adequate health insurance for medical and dental care*

- *Encouragement to work a reasonable number of hours and to maintain a healthy balance between work and family life*

- *Parental/family leave for birth or adoption or family emergencies*

- *Adequate retirement program*

- *Support for spiritual health—personal "Sabbath" time (usually not on Sunday morning for church workers)*

- *Flexible workplace and flexible work schedules*

- *Confidential help for special problems (so that they can be dealt with promptly and in healthy ways)*

- *Paid vacation and encouragement to take it*

- *Job ("ministry") training and educational support to keep up with rapid change*

The temptation for church members to complain that they do not receive similar benefits in their jobs will be great. Put that on the table. Be upfront about what may be absolutely true. That really isn't the core issue. The greater issue is how the church and Christians serve as a model for the world. Do we want those who serve us to be models, and will we support that?

A healthy family ministry support system recognizes the risks pastors and commissioned ministers face and does not let unrealistic expectations or neglect go unchallenged. These people are valuable human blessings, gifts God has entrusted to our care. He expects us to be good stewards.

DCE Jill Hasstedt serves at Zion Lutheran Church in Belleville, Illinois, where she directs leadership and assimilation ministries.

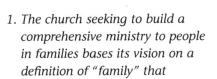

B A S I C S

1. The church seeking to build a comprehensive ministry to people in families bases its vision on a definition of "family" that

- *is true to biblical teaching;*
- *has a legal basis;*
- *focuses on family relationships and responsibilities at different stages of the life cycle; and*
- *corresponds to common usage.*

2. The church seeking to build a comprehensive ministry to people in families is an advocate for children in promoting the interests of the family as a whole.

3. The church seeking to build a comprehensive ministry to people in families takes seriously the development of ministry structures targeted toward singles in promoting the interests of the family as a whole.

4. The church seeking to build a comprehensive ministry to people in families structures worship opportunities that are friendly to people at different stages in the life cycle.

5. The church seeking to build a comprehensive ministry to families recognizes it has unique responsibilities in programming, planning, and scheduling. It promotes the idea that families should be good stewards of their time and that includes "staying home together."

6. The church seeking to build a comprehensive ministry to families focuses its efforts heavily on primary prevention, recognizing the importance of helping families learn skills that will enhance family security and the quality of family life.

7. The church seeking to build a comprehensive ministry to families recognizes that it must help parents see Christ as the center of their home and His church as a caring and supportive community in which Christ-centered values taught at home will be supported and acted upon. It will actively support families in the important role of passing on the faith to the next generation.

8. The church seeking to build a comprehensive ministry to people in families actively seeks to empower its people and to involve them in servanthood beyond its own walls.

9. The church seeking to build a comprehensive ministry to families models family-friendly policies for its own workers and is a leader in doing so in our society.

10. Churches seeking to build a comprehensive ministry to people in families targets educational and relational programming to reach people at times when marker events are occurring in their lives.

Adapted from *Reweaving the Web for Families,* copyright © 1994 Jill Hasstedt. Used with permission.

building a support network

support chart

Leg 1 Support Chart

(Make additions or deletions to make these areas fit your setting.)

Crises

- [ ] Marriage crisis
- [ ] Critical illness
- [ ] Serious injury
- [ ] Foreclosure
- [ ] Adolescent issues
- [ ] Crime victim
- [ ] Divorce
- [ ] Bankruptcy
- [ ] Death
- [ ] Spiritual crisis
- [ ] Job loss
- [ ] Arrest
- [ ] Military deployment of a spouse

Support Congregation May Currently Provide:

- [ ] *hospital visitation*
- [ ] *pastoral counseling*
- [ ] *Stephen Ministry**
- [ ] *referral*
- [ ] *parenting classes*
- [ ] *church library*
- [ ] *specialized small groups*
- [ ] *food pantry*
- [ ] *prayer chain*
- [ ] *alms fund*
- [ ] *transportation*

Life Changes

- [ ] Pregnancy
- [ ] Birth of a child
- [ ] School entry
- [ ] First adolescent
- [ ] Marriage
- [ ] Empty nest
- [ ] Remarriage
- [ ] Caring for elderly parents
- [ ] Divorce
- [ ] Retirement

Support Congregation May Currently Provide:

- [ ] *hospital visitation*
- [ ] *pastoral counseling*
- [ ] *Prepare-Enrich Program**
- [ ] *Stephen Ministry**
- [ ] *referral*
- [ ] *cradle roll*
- [ ] *parenting classes*
- [ ] *specialized support groups*
- [ ] *ChristCare (Stephen Ministry)**
- [ ] *prayer chain*
- [ ] *older adult group*
- [ ] *Milestones**

Special Issues

- [ ] Living together
- [ ] Mental health
- [ ] Chronic illness
- [ ] Substance abuse
- [ ] Job loss
- [ ] Criminal activity/ arrest
- [ ] Church crisis
- [ ] Physical or sexual abuse
- [ ] Debt management

Support Congregation May Currently Provide:

- [ ] *Bible classes*
- [ ] *referral*
- [ ] *community resources*
- [ ] *food pantry*
- [ ] *alms fund*
- [ ] *pastoral care and visitation*
- [ ] *small groups*
- [ ] *Angel Tree*
- [ ] *prison ministry or chaplain*

* See Resources

BASICS

Referral Screening Form

Provider: _____

Date information last updated: _____

Location: _____

Phone: _____

Hours of operation: _____

Cost and availability of sliding scale fees: _____

Counselor Certification and Affiliation

- [ ] *Look for MSW (masters of social work)*
- [ ] *AAMFT (American Association of Marriage and Family Therapists)*
- [ ] *Doctor of Psychology or Psychiatry*
- [ ] *AACC (American Association of Christian Counselors)*
- [ ] *ACA (American Counseling Association)*
- [ ] *Other:* _____

Biographical information (counselor and staff): where trained, experience, etc. _____

_____

List specialization(s): substance abuse, marriage, ADD, etc.

_____

- [ ] *Support for evangelical, conservative Christian values: abortion and right-to-life views, sanctity of marriage, do they pray with clients, do they use biblical support in counseling, faith background*

Health care companies they accept or for which they are preferred providers:

_____

_____

_____

Specific information required from client:
- [ ] *proof of income or employment* [ ] *Social Security card*
- [ ] *family data* [ ] *birth certificates* [ ] *insurance card*
- [ ] *utility bills* [ ] *rent receipts* [ ] *service record* [ ] *credit-card bills*
- [ ] *other* _____

- [ ] *Reputation for quality service*

building a support network

Agency Referral Form

Other Support and Assistance Programs

_____

_____

_____

_____

_____

_____

_____

Detailed List of Services Available from This Group or Agency

_____

_____

_____

_____

_____

_____

Eligibility Information and How to Access

_____

_____

_____

_____

_____

_____

_____

Other Notes

_____

_____

_____

_____

_____

_____

_____

Appendix Option

Local Lutheran Church

Policy on Adult Emergency Information Forms

1. General Policy: Background

An authorized person shall have a list of emergency contact information for all adults as well as minors on trips more then 60 miles from the church.

2. Background

Adults can have emergencies too: heart attacks, accidents, stroke. While a spouse or close family member may be present, that person may be incapacitated or unable to think clearly in a crisis.

3. Policy Guidelines

a. A designated leader will distribute and then collect emergency information forms prior to leaving.

b. The form should include an emergency contact person (someone not on the trip) and contact information (phone, cell phone, etc.).

c. The form should include medical conditions or allergies that might affect emergency treatment.

d. Adults are encouraged to have insurance information and lists of medications they are taking with them at all times. This encouragement should be included in advance information for all trips.

4. Originally prepared by _____

5. Date prepared: _____

6. Date approved: _____

7. Dates revised: _____

building a support network

Resources

Print Resources

Right from the Start by Shirley K. Morgenthaler. CPH (order no. 12-4090).

Teaching Your Children Christian Values by Kay Meyer.

Life in the Sandwich Generation by Kay L. Meyer.

FAITHfully Parenting Preschoolers by John R. Bucka. CPH (order no. 12-4137).

FAITHfully Parenting Tweens by John R. Bucka. CPH (order no. 12-4189).

FAITHfully Parenting Teens by John R. Bucka. CPH (order no. 12-4114).

Web Resources

www.youthandfamilyinstitute.org. The Youth and Family Institute provides helpful information and resources for those involved in family ministy including Milestones, FaithChest, and other programs that celebrate a child's faith journey. Dedicated to Christ-centered family issues.

www.stephenministries.com. Stephen Ministries offers resources and training for comprehensive small-group ministry, including focused care within groups. Provides resources and training for personalized support and one-to-one lay caring in congregations.

www.search-institute.org. Research-based information and tools for helping children develop "Assets" (sets of strengths) that prevent risk-taking behavior.

www.lea.org. Lutheran Education Association provides various resources, including the DCENet, a list serve for directors of Christian education.

www.prepare-enrich.com. Prepare/Enrich includes a marriage preparation and enrichment program administered by trained counselors, pastors, and church professionals. From Life Innovations—Marriage Preparation Programs.

www.lcms.org. Visit The Lutheran Church—Missouri Synod Family Ministry Office for information on the Lutheran Family Ministry Network.

www.familyshieldministries.com. Family Shield Ministries is an agency concerned with providing support for families and those who minister to families.

www.lutheransforlife.org. Lutherans For Life provides comprehensive pro-life information and support for families.

www.family.org. This extensive Web site of Focus on the Family and its well-know leader, Dr. James Dobson, is filled with information and resources available through Focus on the Family.

Basics